educational
psychology

Studies in the
Postmodern Theory of Education

Joe L. Kincheloe and Shirley R. Steinberg
General Editors

Vol. 95

PETER LANG
New York • Washington, D.C./Baltimore • Bern
Frankfurt am Main • Berlin • Brussels • Vienna • Oxford

Suzanne Gallagher

educational
psychology

DISRUPTING THE
DOMINANT DISCOURSE

PETER LANG
New York • Washington, D.C./Baltimore • Bern
Frankfurt am Main • Berlin • Brussels • Vienna • Oxford

Library of Congress Cataloging-in-Publication Data

Gallagher, Suzanne.
Educational psychology: disrupting the dominant discourse / Suzanne Gallagher.
p. cm. — (Counterpoints: vol. 95)
Includes bibliographical references and index.
1. Educational psychology. 2. Critical pedagogy. I. Title.
II. Counterpoints (New York, N. Y.) ; vol. 95.
LB1051 .G2175   370.15—dc21   00050657
ISBN 0-8204-4130-9
ISSN 1058-1634

Bibliographic information published by **Die Deutsche Bibliothek**.
Die Deutsche Bibliothek lists this publication in the 'Deutsche
Nationalbibliografie'; detailed bibliographic data is available
on the Internet at http://dnb.ddb.de

Cover design by Lisa Barfield

The paper in this book meets the guidelines for permanence and durability
of the Committee on Production Guidelines for Book Longevity
of the Council of Library Resources.

Printed in the United States of America

Contents

Introduction

The work presented in this book reflects a shift in thinking about the discipline of educational psychology. Traditionally, a discipline like educational psychology is considered to be a neutral, objective, scientifically validated body of knowledge. Those involved with education understand this knowledge as potentially useful as it enables effective action in the teaching-learning process. Many understand educational psychology as potentially working in the interest of ameliorating the current crisis in education. A promissory note (Soyland, 1994) is offered to preservice teachers regarding their learning the discipline, i.e., if you learn this material, if it becomes a part of you, you will be a better teacher.

However, I am skeptical about the knowledge of the discipline and the promises it extends to its students. Rather than a neutral, objective, scientifically validated body of knowledge, I espouse the perspective that all knowledge, including scientific knowledge, is the result of social processes. Knowledge is produced through social negotiations by persons in particular contexts, who have histories and biases, and who are embedded in power relations. The "truth" of the discipline has as much to do with social and political issues as it has to do with science.

I worry about what goes on as students, usually preservice teachers, "learn" educational psychology. Are students learning about the complex processes of schooling, to think critically and ethically? Is it *learning* that is going on in classes of educational psychology? Or is what is going on actually *enculturation* into a particular meaning-making system (Doyle & Carter, 1996) that generally takes place in introductory courses? Students of the discipline are encouraged to internalize the technical rationality in which teaching and learning are reduced to technical issues or problems. "Critical" thinking may be encouraged, but it is often thinking that is locked within the confines of a particular paradigm.

In this book I "talk back" (hooks, 1989) to the discourse of the discipline of educational psychology. I question the common-sense, the taken-for-granted notions of the discipline and I resist and contest its scientific reasoning. I strive to move against the traditional reading that accepts the reasoning that too often is used as justification to explain and legitimize why some children benefit from their educational experience and others do not.

This work started as an uneasy reading of the discipline. It became clear to me that only a narrow body of "knowledge" was allowed into the discussion of educational psychology. Material that questioned or contradicted the mainstream discourse was often ignored or regarded as "soft," flawed, or unscientific. This was most perplexing as I found the counterdiscourse more interesting, more "rational," and much more concerned with issues of justice. I became engaged in a critical perspective.

In this book I exhibit a stance of Foucauldian skepticism regarding the "neutral" tenants of the discipline of educational psychology. Rather than ameliorating the crisis in education, I see educational psychology implicated in the crisis through its knowledge base and practices. I interrogate the discourse of the discipline as a "regime of truth" (Foucault, 1980a), a nexus of power, knowledge, and social control.

I am in an unusual position by my espousal of this perspective because I consider myself a student of the discipline. Even so, taking a critical, oppositional stance regarding the discipline of educational psychology as a neutral body of knowledge places me "against" the discipline in a sense. I have asked myself the question: Why can't I just do what I am supposed to do within the accepted boundaries of educational research regarding educational psychology? Why not remain within what Said (1994) represents as the acceptable and "responsible mainstream." For me remaining within the mainstream of the discipline is an untenable position.

The work that I take up here is self-consciously political. This work is driven by the question of Cicero, "Cui bono?" Who benefits? (Star, 1991). The question means that I need to ask, "Whom does this discourse serve?" (Foucault, 1980a). Who is it who benefits from the work that I do, or the discourse I interrogate or espouse? I maintain that the discourse of educational psychology primarily supports the knowledge, beliefs, values, and power positions of the dominant middle-class Anglo perspective in U.S. society. I am troubled and moved to action by the harm that is done daily to students who do not conform to the established "norm" sanctioned by the discipline.

This position does not necessarily ingratiate me in the "profession." Said (1994) is helpful here as I appropriate his notion of the work I do as a form of *amateurism*, i.e., this work is activity animated by care and affection. An *amateur*, in this sense, is one who understands that as a concerned member of the society they may, they must, raise questions about moral, ethical, philosophical issues. This focus is broader than the technical concerns of the discipline. This work is taken up in the spirit of democratizing the discipline of educational psychology, allowing multiple perspectives to engage the rationale, constructs, and issues underpinning it. The book's aim is to ask questions about the discipline in the hope that the educational experience of all students can be more liberatory and ultimately more just.

In chapter 1, I discuss the discipline of educational psychology from multiple viewpoints. The discourse frequently expresses different and conflicting perspectives regarding its position and potential to advance teacher education. However, educational psychology generally enjoys the status of an authoritarian body of neutral knowledge that can be used to enhance the teaching-learning process. I counter this mainstream view through analyzing the discourse of the discipline as a "regime of truth" (Foucault, 1980a). A brief introduction of postmodern critique is explained in terms of key issues: meaning, language, and discourse; the formation of subjectivities; relations of power and knowledge.

Chapter 2 gathers examples of counterdiscursive feminist scholarship. Counterdiscourses are presented as a way of "talking back" to mainstream discourses of literature and science. The selection of work highlights the metaphors of location, vision, and voice and helps to situate the work that follows.

There are two aspects of "methods" in research that are articulated in chapter 3. First, methodology refers to the intellectual means utilized to conduct this research activity. I offer an explanation of why the methodologies of traditional educational research (particularly that of educational psychology), and their respective epistemologies, are inadequate for research aimed at educational reform. Second, important strategies that are used in the critical method I utilize, i.e., discourse analysis, are discussed.

Chapter 4 takes up an analysis of educational psychology through a critical reading of the discipline. I examine the particular rationality of its discourse as well as its nondiscursive aspects. Educational psychology is based on the modernist ideology of technical rationality with its potential to predict and control. This rationality is often unexpressed and unexamined, and therefore it needs to be clarified and made problematic. There are several nondiscursive aspects of the discipline where knowledge and power come together and implicate each other. These nondiscursive forces of the discipline include the political, social, historical, and economic contexts that embed the discipline. Questions are discussed, such as: Who is authorized to speak for the discipline? Whose knowledge is promoted as the "truth" of the discipline? How is it that misrepresentations continue to be accepted in its discourse?

Chapter 5 discusses how power, scientific knowledge, and control of bodies are characteristic of modern disciplines. Through "technologies of power" (Foucault, 1995), i.e., hierarchical observation, normalizing gaze, examination, that emanate from and support the dominant discourse of educational psychology students are formed and "marked" by their conformity to the "norm." Technologies of power are evident in the everyday, taken-for-granted practices of the discourse. Disciplinary technologies create the "normalizing gaze" that is explicated and critiqued in this chapter.

In chapter 6, I supply examples of how I struggle to develop my praxis. It is an illustration of the issues important to a critical stance toward the discipline's discourse in courses related to educational psychology. Through questioning and intertextual reading, it is possible to open a space where students can engage issues in their social, political, and epistemological complexity. This is a way of making the familiar strange (Foucault, 1995) so that the everyday assumptions and practices of the discipline can be more easily questioned and changed. This chapter presents a call for critical literacy regarding the discipline's knowledge claims and practices. From this critical stance, the work of the discipline becomes more reflexive and has the potential of being more socially just.

CHAPTER 1

Multiple Readings of the Discipline of Educational Psychology

> *People know what they do;*
> *they frequently know why they do what they do;*
> *but what they don't know is what what they do does.*
> (Foucault, quoted in Dreyfus & Rabinow, 1983, p. 187)

A Story

It was my first class as teacher of an educational psychology course. My enthusiasm had been growing as I prepared for the class. I was eager to engage my students not only in learning the content of the discipline, but also to help them become conscious of their experience as we "did" educational psychology through the class process. In other words, I wanted the course to be a space where we would study educational psychology and raise consciousness of the practice of it at the same time. This seemed a worthwhile goal to pursue as I believed it would add to the relevancy of the coursework for the students, most of whom were preservice teachers.

We were reading through the syllabus with a nice amount of discussion, checking understanding, asking questions. The excitement I felt seemed matched by the students as we engaged the coursework for the first time. We came to the course requirements, and I explained how the grades would be determined. The giving of "grades"[1] was an aspect of the class that I had thought over seriously. "Grades" or "marks" had meant much to me as a student; I assumed that the grading system would be equally as important to my first class of educational psychology students. I was eager for my students to be successful, and their understanding the grading system would help them meet the requirements of the course. It seemed fairly simple: I took the responsibility to ensure that the material was presented effectively, and that the marking system was clear and fair; each student's effort would complete the equation for success.

Then it happened. I had included a series of "pop quizzes" that would account for 50% of the grade. One student raised her hand. "Why 'pop' quizzes?" she inquired. I welcomed the question. It was perfect really in that use of the "pop quiz" was a clear example of how we could connect the content and process of the course. My response included two concepts that we would study in the course: first, the usefulness of the classic "variable-interval" reinforcement schedule; and, second, the effectiveness of "spaced" over "massed" study. I explained that because students never knew when the quiz would occur they would be "motivated" to study as the course went along. I assured the students that the material on the quiz would be nothing tricky or obscure as it would come from what they had read or what we had discussed in class; there was no need for them to become overly concerned. Actually, I insisted, I was doing them a favor as "studies show" that there is much more long-term learning following study that is spread out over time rather than study that is "massed" as happens when students cram for tests. I didn't allow myself to entertain the remembrance of a conversation that I had with a colleague while preparing the course. The associate had assured me that I had to do something to make sure the students came to class and studied. She used pop quizzes, and I decided to do the same.

I was satisfied, actually pleased, with my response to the student's inquiry. "Okay?" I asked. It was not okay. The student said that she felt trapped. She described herself as a serious student, but there might be a time when she has to miss class. What if it was on a day when there was a pop quiz? I had stated in the syllabus that quizzes could not be made up, but that I would drop the lowest mark. The lowest mark could be an "F" if she had to miss a quiz. "Did that help?" Her expression revealed that it really didn't, but the student thanked me for my answer. The rest of the students seemed to accept my rationale, and there were no further questions on the topic. The class continued.

Later that evening I reflected on the happenings of the class. It seemed as though we were off to a great start. Then I pictured the student who had presented me with the opportunity to explain the "pop quiz" aspect of the grading system. I had a degree of certainty both in that the answer I gave was grounded in the discipline under study, and in the "effectiveness" of the practice I had explained. Gradually, the initial pleasure that I felt gave way to embarrassment. The student had seen other dimensions in the practice of "pop quizzes." In one sense the "case was closed." I was the teacher; my decisions were well thought out and benevolent. However, the student had resisted my rationale by facing the unequal power relationship between teacher and student and by questioning the grading practice. In the process of questioning she had exposed an example of "what what we do does." The scientific knowledge of the discipline of educational psychology justified the use of pop quizzes to exert control over the students to attend class and to study. Through the student's objection and my reflection on my practice I realized that my answer was not nearly so important as the questions that had arisen in the student and in myself.

This story serves as an appropriate beginning for this book for several reasons. First, it highlights the autobiographical aspect of research in general and of this work in particular. Foucault (1988) has said that, "Each of my works is a part of my own biography. For one or another reason I had the occasion to feel and live those things" (p. 11). Similarly, those who read this work do, in some sense, read me.

This work is part of my own biography in that rethinking the discipline of educational psychology and disrupting its dominant discourse began with my own uneasy reading (Apple, 1993) of mainstream educational psychology texts. Through a critical reading and analysis of the discipline I began to understand that much of what I had accepted as "objective," "neutral," and "stable" in the discipline is actually a product of social negotiations (Gergen, 1985) and "reflection of conventions" (Kincheloe, 1993) imbued with political interests. This book is an opportunity for me to affirm my right, but more important, my responsibility to read, understand, and transform (Freire & Macedo, 1987; Giroux, 1987) my experience of both teaching and learning educational psychology.

Second, the story demonstrates the "relational" aspect of education. Schooling is primarily and in multiple ways relational (Apple, 1996). The relational aspects extend beyond student-to-teacher and student-to-student relationships. The work that I am presenting includes the interrogation of power relationships that exist throughout educational institutions: how students are judged and sorted and against what/whose norms; what/whose knowledge is of most value; who may speak and when. I also study the relationships among power, knowledge, and social control. I am interested in the relationship of the mainstream theoretical perspectives of the discipline's discourse and the everyday practices of education that both limit and constrain education. When oppressive perspectives and processes are recognized, it is possible to resist and contest them in order to support a more emancipatory pedagogy concerned with a critical and democratic social order. I argue that the relation of what is said and done in the name of the discipline marks educational psychology as a "site of struggle" (Aronowitz & Giroux, 1991).

Third, the story highlights the significance of the act of questioning, my own and this student's. Questioning is a means of critical examination that aims to problematize the discipline, i.e., to question what has been taken for granted (Foucault, 1984). In particular, this book is a vehicle of questioning the commonly accepted view of educational psychology as a neutral field of study. Thus, the work that follows is an interrogation of the very specialized scientific and technical discipline of educational psychology.

Fourth, the story positions this work as a postmodern critique. A postmodern critique is "a different way of seeing and working, rather than a fixed body of ideas, a clearly worked-out position or a set of critical methods and techniques" (Usher & Edwards, 1994, p. 2). A major concern of this book is the interrogating and thinking about the discipline's theoretical perspectives in their complexity. In modernity, theory provides the foundation supporting the logic of scientific methodology and its interest in prediction, explanation, and control. Theory holds quite an "allure" for educationalists in general (G. Thomas, 1997), and educational psychologists in particular, as in contemporary teacher education programs where it is taken up and used in the interest of technical progress. Contrastingly, my intention is to theorize in a way that helps in understanding the present predicament in education, and where possible and necessary critically engage it so that the discipline can be transformed (hooks, 1994).

A postmodern critique of the discourse does not mean that the discourse of the discipline of educational psychology is not taken seriously. On the contrary, it is too powerful not to be taken seriously; constructive criticism is a clear indication that the discourse is taken seriously (Apple, 1996). In a sense, the discourse itself invites critical analysis because every discourse is a "stumbling block . . . a point of resistance and a starting point for an opposing strategy (Foucault, 1990, p. 10). In this sense the dominant discourse of educational psychology can even be considered *useful* as it provides an opportunity for interrogation and disruption.

The openings that result from this disruption provide a space where the reimagining of educational psychology can take place, and ethical conversations and a language of possibilities can be engaged (Giroux, 1992; Welch, 1990).[2] Jennifer Gore (1993) reminds us of Foucault's admonition to identify "spaces of freedom" that are possible as we become aware of oppressive effects that underlie the seemingly neutral practices of a modern discipline like educational psychology. My student in the story certainly provided a disruption for me and consequently a space for the exercise of freedom.

A Mainstream Reading:
Educational Psychology as Promissory Note

Educational psychology generally is regarded as a discipline concerned with the multifaceted issues of the teaching-learning process. Today, the influence of the discipline is obvious as its practices, knowledge base, research, and conceptual frameworks pervade educational discussions.

Many members of the educational psychology community are optimistic regarding the status of the field and the potential educational psychology has in helping to improve the teaching-learning process in our schools. In fact, a certain optimism pervades many claims of the discipline exemplifying the metaphor of "promissory note." This rhetorical device, frequently used in scientific discourse, conveys to the reader a factual status of the text and the proposed reward for "buying into" the particular thesis established by the text (Soyland, 1994).

For example, it has been noted that the field "seems to have come of age, it has matured, it is sophisticated, it is pretty independent from other fields and areas of psychology" (Salomon, 1995, p. 105). The authors of the celebrated *Handbook of Educational Psychology* (Berliner & Calfee, 1996) assert that: "It is clear that our field has been and continues to be highly productive and remarkably influential. Its findings, concepts, methods, and points of view are widely adopted by scholars in other disciplines and cross a wide range of research and evaluation activities. . . . The field is alive and growing" (p. 1020). The newsletter for members of the American Psychological Association (APA) Division 15, Educational Psychology (November 1996), contains some confident messages to the President of the United States and members of the Congress as they face legislative decisions on education:

> [Educational psychologists] have developed and tested various theories, and have come to some important decisions about what works in the classrooms. . . . and what doesn't work and why. . . . We are the backbone of education, and the basis for many other important fields. . . . Every legislator should have an educational psychologist on staff as a consultant and resource! (Neeley, 1996, p. 1)

Wittrock (1992) is confident that: "[educational psychology] can become recognized as a core field of psychology, responsible for contributing to the creation of psychological theory, to knowledge and research about education, and reciprocally, through research and development, to the understanding and improvement of education" (p. 140). Anita Woolfolk (1995), eminent author of educational psychology textbooks, obviously agrees with this evaluation. She explains to her readers who are preservice teachers that "if you can become a more expert learner by applying the knowledge from this text . . . then you will be a better teacher as well" (p. 10).

However, despite these waves of optimism, educational psychologists are simultaneously embroiled in debate. Many of these debates are centered on the place of the discipline in discussions of school reform and teacher education. There exists the contrasting perception of educational psychology as a "field

marked by little definitional consensus, many theoretical per-
suasions, and diversified scholarship" (Walberg & Haertel, 1992,
p. 6). Furthermore, although the diversity of the field is considered positive by many, some complain that "the field of educational psychology does not have much of a core" (Salomon, 1995,
p. 105). It has been noted that the "closing decades of the twentieth century have seen many challenges to the hegemony of educational psychology as the 'master science'" (Berliner & Calfee,
1996, p. 1020). Others have expressed a sense of "growing awareness among educational psychologists of the need to reexamine
their own discipline" (Peterson, Clark, & Dickson, 1990, p. 524).
It has even been asked if educational psychology "as a discipline
is on the verge of extinction" (Grinder, 1989, p. 4).

Some of the discrepancy in the views presented above may be
explained by recognizing that arguments vary according to the intended audience and who is speaking. There are multiple voices
within the discipline; many are positive and optimistic about the
discipline's potential to help ameliorate the crisis in education
when policy makers are addressed. When talking to each other,
however, educational psychologists tend to be more frank in discussing the problematics of the discipline's tenets, although some
assume a defensive position regarding the discipline's potential
and value to the field of education.

When considering curriculum issues, especially for introductory courses, there is an escalating debate regarding the content,
process, and goals of the coursework. For example, some recognized experts in the field (e.g., Woolfolk, 1995, 1996) encourage
the traditional image of the field as "foundational," emphasizing
mastery of the content of the discipline as helping preservice
teachers be better teachers. Others assert that the discipline is
more of a "resource" (Blumenfeld & Anderson, 1996), assisting
preservice teachers in their reflections on the teaching-learning
process.

Regardless of this debate educational psychology's discourse
generally is presented as an authoritarian and neutral body of
knowledge that can guide educational practice and facilitate better learning. The current mainstream educational process in this
country, in which this discourse is embedded, is organized
around the modernist project, i.e., it celebrates reason and the individual subject, and has faith that a neutral science promotes
progress, certainty, order, efficiency, and control. The discipline

of educational psychology, based in a technical rationality, is concerned with advancing these modern purposes.

There is an alternative way of looking at modernity's project and the human science of educational psychology in particular. As critique, the alternative perspective maintains a skeptical stance regarding the discipline as a neutral body of knowledge. This perspective is influenced by Michel Foucault's concern with how modern societies exert control over human persons through the practices and knowledge claims of modern sciences.

An Alternative Reading:
Educational Psychology as a "Regime of Truth"

The ideas of Michel Foucault (1926–1984) are helpful in the work I undertake throughout this book. I accept his invitation to use his ideas as "little toolboxes . . . [so one can] open them and make use of such and such a sentence or idea, of one analysis or another, as they would a screwdriver or a monkey wrench" (Foucault, quoted in Eribon, 1991, p. 237). Using Foucault's tool, understanding discourses as *regimes of truth*,[3] I believe it is possible to analyze the discourse of educational psychology in a "critical" manner.

Foucault is skeptical regarding modern disciplines, especially those connected with education (Ball, 1990). Foucault's position is that the discourse of the modern disciplines is a nexus of power and knowledge. Power and knowledge imply each other, as Foucault (1995) explains "there is no power relation without the correlative constitution of a field of knowledge, nor any knowledge that does not presuppose and constitute at the same time power relations" (p. 27). Although we think of the knowledge of modern sciences as being "discovered," there is something else going on beside/underneath the scientific and objective process of discovery. The knowledge or "truth" of the discipline is developed though a series of power relations. Foucault (1980a) explains that there are "mechanisms and instances which enable one to distinguish true and false statements, the means by which each is sanctioned; the techniques and procedures accorded value in the acquisition of truth; the status of those who are charged with saying what counts as true" (p. 131).

Educational psychology is a fine example of this nexus of

power and knowledge. Educational psychologists know what is true and acceptable within the meaning-making system of the discipline. They have privileged the scientific method as a means to access the truth, and become skilled at experiments of prediction and control. In fact, one has only to review the Board of Consulting Editors of any journal in the field to ascertain who is "charged with saying what counts as true."

Foucault has pointed out that it is through regimes of power that modern societies control their populations; the discourse of educational psychology is a regime through which students and teachers alike are controlled. Persons are "disciplined," albeit in subtle and often invisible ways, through the discipline's knowledge claims and practices. Some might argue that this is the benign practice of socialization. However, the objective is the production of students and teachers of a particular kind, i.e., docile and useful (Foucault, 1995). The norms used as the standard in assessing these qualities, although considered objective, are arbitrary and in fact favor members of the dominant group in the society over members of subaltern groups.

Through an analysis that takes seriously the relation of power and knowledge in the formation of the modern sciences, it is possible to see the discipline differently; to "make the familiar strange" as Foucault (1995) says. When that which is so familiar, taken for granted, is looked at differently, we are able to see its "underside" and understand what else is going on through the production and consumption of the discipline's discourse. We are able to contest and resist the discipline's power that has uneven and often deleterious effects on students who are subjected to its tenets.

Understanding the discourse, what is said and done in the name of the discipline, of educational psychology as a regime of truth complicates and disturbs the commonsense understanding of power and knowledge. We usually accept that "knowledge is power," or knowledge gives a person power. In this sense then, preservice teachers acquire power to be better teachers through learning the knowledge/truth of the discipline of educational psychology, "If you learn this information—you will be a better teacher." The position I take is an oppositional stance regarding the mainstream reading of the discipline; it is a critique of the discourse, presenting a kind of counterdiscourse, a counterhegemonic discourse. I take a position that is both within the discipline and against the discipline.[4] I want to raise questions concerning the discipline's "dominant discourse" as it is perceived as neutral, authoritarian, and positive. The work of this book is situated within radical/critical/feminist educational perspectives that assert the need to question accepted truths and assumptions about education and the society in which it is embedded (Weiler, 1992). Implicit in this approach is a commitment to and belief that knowledge "in its present and past formations and branches, could have been, and may yet be, constituted in other ways. Our relation to facts, disciplines, departments, and hierarchies of knowledge is less natural or normal than concocted, and thus alterable" (Leitch, 1996, p. 76).

Through a critical reading and analysis of the discourse presented in two textbooks[5] nominated by the educational psychology community as "classic,"[6] I argue with many of the discursive elements of the discipline's discourse. For instance, I will show that the *technical rationality* characteristic of the discourse that provides an organizational resource for the discipline also constrains because it limits the thinking, questioning, "reasoning," and "practice" of educators.

From a perspective of technical rationality the crisis in education is viewed as a series of technical problems that need to be solved. The metaphor of teacher as "technician" is operative in this perspective. What can teachers *do* to improve, control, or ameliorate the teaching-learning process? It's a question of technique, using the most effective technique, and using the technique effectively. This metaphor must be contrasted with other views of the teacher, for example, the teacher as transformative intellectual (Giroux & McLaren, 1996). Teacher as transformative intellectual presents "a critical view of teacher work and authority . . . one consistent with the principles and practice of democracy" (p. 305).

This more radical/critical perspective allows for different types of questions, questions beyond technique. Questions regarding educational crisis and reform need to be connected to a "wider discourse of freedom and democratic struggle" (Giroux & McLaren, 1989, p. xviii). Working from this perspective, I intend to identify problematic issues embedded in the assurances made by the discourse of educational psychology, and the "scientific" formulation of disciplinary principles. Here matters at a "macro" level of ideology and institutions are examined. However, and perhaps more important, I am also concerned with situations at the "micro" level regarding the everyday practices of schooling that are authorized by the discourse.

Critical Discourse Analysis

Critical discourse analysis is explored in more depth in chapter 3; however, a brief discussion of this model's perspective may be helpful here. Critical discourse analysis is a mode of examination, a way of looking at, and asking questions about anything *textual.* Textual is used here in both the "narrow conventional sense of written texts and in the much broader sense of any discourses, practices, institutions . . . any structure generally which is productive of signification"[7] (Usher & Edwards, 1994, p. 18). Given this description, it is a mode of *poststructural analysis.* The key aspect of this analysis is that it is a means of interrogating traditional understandings of (a) meaning, language, discourse (b) subjectivity, and (c) power relationships in knowledge production. These will be mentioned briefly below, as they are key factors throughout this book.

Language—Reflecting and Clear?

Traditionalists see *meanings* in language and discourse as fixed. Meaning in language *reflects* an objective reality; it emanates from the interior essence of the object. Language is believed to function as "simple transmitters of information from writer to reader" (Madigan, Johnson, & Linton, 1995, p. 433).

Critical discourse analysis, on the other hand, stresses that language and discourse *constitute* reality. Meanings are never fixed; they are influenced by the multiplicity of issues that form the context in which they are used. "Meaning" in this perspective is understood as exterior to the object; it is inscribed and contingent. Words that describe concepts can be appreciated as "social artifacts" that acquire their meaning depending on how they are used, not from any reference point in the "real" world (Gergen, 1985).

Therefore, meaning in a discipline's discourse is not fixed; rather meaning is "shaped contextually within institutions and by prevailing social practices" (Bensimon, 1995, p. 597). Gergen (1985) explains that a certain understanding is sustained and may prevail through time not because of "the empirical validity of the perspective in question, but on the vicissitudes of social processes (e.g., communication, negotiation, conflict, rhetoric)" (p. 268).

Constructing Subjects: Subjectification

Traditionally persons are understood as autonomous, coherent individuals. We speak of "subjects" as having certain natural and essential characteristics, e.g., intelligent, motivated. These individuals, our subjects, are seen as emerging through the dynamic interaction of their biological development and their social reality, and within their own history. In traditional research studies effort is exerted toward discovering some "truth" about the subject or subjects, or the human person in general.

However, there also exists a very different understanding of "subject." Subjects are regarded as constituted, and constantly reconstituted (Usher & Edwards, 1994; Weedon, 1987) by the discursive practices to which they are subjected. "Subjectivity" is the product of society, a human reality and social construction (Sarup, 1993). Subjectification is understood as the process by which a subject is made an "object." This represents so much of the work of educational psychology with its focus on measuring individual differences of students, placement of students along the normal curve, and ever-increasing categories of differentiation. The categories of differences among students are often accepted without a critical examination of what the category means or in spite of ambiguity. For example, the "normal" versus "abnormal," or "exceptional" versus "gifted" categorizations of children.

The goal of research within a critical perspective then clashes with traditional research in educational psychology. A critical research perspective is not concerned with discovering a "truth" about the subject, rather the "re-search" aims to understand something different about students. The focus shifts to the social, historical, and political contexts in which subjects are constructed as they are (Prado, 1995; Usher & Edwards, 1994).

Power Relations: The Authority to Name

As was stated earlier, schooling is relational. Power relations pervade the schooling process and are discernable in a variety of sites. The commonsense understanding of power is that it is a commodity that can be possessed. One "has" power, and can exercise it in relation to others. Power is often understood as "power over"; it flows from a centralized source, and from top to bottom (Sawicki, 1991). Power, in this sense, can be considered repressive or inhibiting.

Foucault (1980a, 1988, 1995) discusses another notion of power that is particularly characteristic of modern power, or modern modalities of power. Foucault's notion is that power is not only repressive, it is also *productive*. Discourses espoused by disciplines are productive in that they constitute the "reality" they present. These discourses are never independent of history, power, and multiple interests.

Power is not a possession, but rather exercised in relations. Power doesn't only flow from a centralized location, but is "capillary" operating at the "lowest extremities of the social body in everyday social practices" (Fraser, 1989, p. 18). Foucault (1980a) explains,

> What makes power hold good, what makes it accepted, is simply the fact that it doesn't only weigh on us as a force that says no, but that it traverses and produces things, it induces pleasure, forms knowledge, produces discourse. It needs to be considered as a productive network which runs through the whole social body, much more than a negative instance whose function is repression. (p. 119)

Foucault asserts (1980a) that in the period we call "modernity" there has been a "veritable technological take-off in the productivity of power" (p. 119). This is not a "power over" but a *power to name* as is found in the human sciences.[8] Power is productive through a discipline in that it "makes individuals; it is the specific technique of power that regards individuals both as objects and as instruments of its exercise" (Foucault, 1995, p. 170).

Again, we draw on Foucault's (1980a) understanding of scientific disciplines as "regimes of truth" in which power and knowledge are inextricably related and implicate each other. The "truth," the knowledge of a discipline, needs to be interrogated as an assembly of facts and techniques that have been "discovered" and accepted by the community through which we come to know individuals (e.g., characterizing some learners as "motivated" or "gifted" and others as "unmotivated" or "average"). The truth of educational psychology needs to be understood in terms of its technologies of power, as an *"ensemble of rules* (emphasis added) according to which that which is considered true or false are separated" (p. 133). Truth is seen as "A system of ordered procedures for the production, regulation, distribution, circulation, and operation of statements. . . . [and is] linked in a circular relation with systems of power which produce and sustain it . . . induce and . . . extend it" (1980a, p. 133).

Through its discourse educational psychology operates to provide increasingly complex categories through which learners and teachers arc subjected to ever-increasing processes of hyperdifferentiation and made objects of investigation, categorization, intervention, and regulation (Usher, 1993).

This unconventional manner of looking at how knowledge and power implicate each other presents quite a shift for educational psychologists. Educational psychologists usually think of the discipline as being "scientifically" produced. It is precisely this assurance of knowing "the world 'scientifically' and 'as it really is' which makes [the discipline's knowledge claims] powerful" (Usher & Edwards, 1994, p. 47). Educational psychology claims that through its ever-increasing technological ability it has the power to *see* students as they really are, and to manipulate the environment for optimal learning.

Critical discourse analysis can subvert this understanding and expose how various categories are the result of human construction and are never free of history, power, and human interest. Thus, what is understood as a "will to knowledge" can mean a "will to power"; to interrogate this "regime" clearly is to enter a political struggle (Foucault, 1980a). This manner of critique can be helpful in identifying areas of struggle in the discipline's discourse and ways of developing strategies for change.

These issues are particularly important to instructors of preservice teachers. What is really happening as we prepare these professionals for their future work? Doyle and Carter (1996) raise this issue of tension regarding what is really going on as "novices become members of practitioner communities" (p. 27). Is the process learning or enculturation? The question of "enculturation" through initiation into a discourse community is not easily settled, nor need it be. What is important is that the tension in these multiple perspectives be recognized, interrogated, and appreciated as part of the contested terrain of the significance of language, epistemology, and critique.

The aim of this book is to apply a critical reading and analysis of the mainstream, dominant discourse of educational psychology. This is significant as educational psychology's mainstream discourse perpetuates powerful ways of thinking about students and everyday teaching practices; these need to be made explicit and interrogated in hope that educationalists can become aware of oppressive, albeit sometimes unintentional, effects of our practices. We can change both our practice and its effects on students.

The time seems right for this kind of work in educational psychology. Educational psychologists do seek to understand the discipline's contribution to the education of preservice teachers (e.g., Anderson et al., 1995; Peterson et al., 1990; Shuell, 1996) and are increasingly direct in their challenge to each other to reflect on what it means to be an educational psychologist. In addition, and perhaps more important, educational psychologists need to ponder the current practices and their effects, as well as the legacy of the discipline. The chapters that follow take up a discussion of these complex issues.

CHAPTER 2

Literature of Transgression

The task of this book is to critically analyze the canon of educational psychology, i.e., the discipline's dominant discourse. I have found that feminist scholarship offers a helpful set of concepts for this analysis. I offer examples of this scholarship in this chapter because I place my work within this intellectual tradition. I refer to the choice of the material included in this chapter as examples of a *literature of transgression.*

I want to relate this chapter to the story that I used to begin chapter 1. My student was contesting my explanation of the grading practices for the class. Although I was presenting what I imagined to be benign and fair procedures, she did not agree. Even when I connected what I was proposing as directly related and validated by educational psychology's discourse she refused my rationalization. My student insisted that her experience of the practice was quite different from the ideal of the rationale embedded in the texts and practices of educational psychology. In effect she was "talking-back," resisting and contesting, transgressing a terrain where students traditionally do not belong. She was questioning the taken-for-granted authority of both teacher and disciplinary discourse. Likewise, much of feminist scholarship questions, talks back, and transgresses the taken-for-granted boundaries of mainstream science.

Including texts from both literature and science may seem peculiar since writing in fields like science and literature is thought to be widely disparate. However, the case has been made that they are not so dissimilar as was once thought (Lyotard, 1993; Soyland, 1994). In this instance the choice has been made for the expression of counterdiscourse that each provides.

The texts I offer here illustrate the importance of voice, positionality, and vision in oppositional activity aimed at interrogating mainstream paradigms. Forms of feminist literary critique, for example, have had the expressed goal of "talking back" (hooks, 1989) to a discourse that sought to contain or silence subaltern voices. Feminist writers have claimed positions on the margins that inform their perspective. The vision that results from this distinct positionality is important to political struggles because it enables seeing things differently.

A feminist critique of science also seeks to present a counter-discourse to mainstream science often considered a colonizing discourse. There is a desire to acknowledge that there are multiple viewpoints, a "heteroglossia" (Bakhtin, 1981), that exist within the scientific community. The metaphor of location likewise is instructive as it influences what is seen, and what may be invisible. This issue of location is discussed in terms of "feminist standpoint" epistemology (Harding, 1991).

Feminist Criticism

Resisting Colonizing Discourse

Resisting colonizing discourses presents a dilemma for feminist authors. Carol Harding (1985) explains "dilemma" as a situation that demands "a choice between conflicting outcomes" (p. 49) by a person who has the "ability to act with intention" (p. 44). Lashgari (1995) characterizes the dilemma of resisting colonizing discourses as a "contrary imperative," that is "to be honest, and to be heard" (p. 1) while discerning that there are serious costs involved in honestly speaking out. The predicament is clear in that there are always those within the dominant group, culture, paradigm who wish to make their perspective normative, and who are determined to silence and/or marginalize anyone who speaks against the dominating force of their discourse.

Foucault (1981) states that all discourse is violence. Feminists have declared discourse that defines them as "Other" as a particular form of discursive violence, and have resisted and contested this violence while recognizing that there are "costs of breaking cultural taboos against speaking out" (Lashgari, 1995, p. 1). Those who lay bare the dominant culture's blindness, contest its universalizing "truth," or refuse its judgment, i.e., those who speak out or "talk back," are perceived by those they offend as "dangerous," as "transgressing."

Lashgari (1995) presents four concepts that can be considered crucial in understanding such transgressive discourse: (a) decentering, (b) heteroglossia, (c) dialogics, and (d) traversia.

The first, "decentering," is a process in which those on the margins speak, contesting their objectification and claiming the position of subject. When this happens, "those who are marginal to the dominant power re-place the center making the margin the new center of their own subjectivity" (p. 2). In claiming this position in which subjects speak for themselves a very different narrative is articulated. Through the act of "naming ourselves and . . . telling our own stories in our own words" (Moraga & Anzaldúa, 1983, p. 23) the colonizers get to hear a voice other than their own with the possibility of releasing them (the colonizers) from their own particular blindness (Lashgari, 1995).

The effects of this decentering process evoke the second concept, "heteroglossia." Heteroglossia occurs when a "multiplicity of voices enters the discourse, when margins talk back to the imperial or neocolonial center" (Lashgari, 1995, p. 3). It is a form of neocolonialism when the dominant power imposes a "monologic definition of truth, and then convinces its members that any deviation would risk chaos" (Lashgari, 1995, p. 11). According to Lashgari, whenever this imposition takes place "there are already numerous voices, subverting, transgressing boundaries, working to disrupt" (p. 11) the colonizer's centralized certitude.

Third, "dialogics" is a constructive discourse that becomes possible "when polyvocal discourse interrupts the dominant monologue" (Lashgari, 1995, p. 3). Lashgari makes a very helpful point that because this discourse is often confrontational and contradictory it is often perceived as a spoiler, as though the confrontational discourse is upsetting a peaceful territory. In actuality, the divisions and discrepancy are always present although unspoken and invisible. Through the dialogic, the interruption of the monologue, a new more inclusive discourse becomes possible.

Fourth, "traversia" is what Lashgari (1995) refers to as a "movement toward understanding" (p. 3). As we move from one narrative to another, from center to margins recognizing multiple centers and perspectives, we participate in a type of transgression of borders. She says that "only by violating the boundaries of the familiar and the proper, risking conflict, can one reach toward connection" (p. 4). It is here that coalitions can be forged.

Teaching as Transgression

bell hooks (1994) takes up the notion of "transgression," the other side of traversia, as the task of teaching. hooks calls for the celebration of the kind of teaching that "enables transgression— a movement against and beyond boundaries" (p. 12). In her work, hooks (1994) is "urging all of us to open our minds and hearts so that we can know beyond the boundaries of what is acceptable, so that we can think, and rethink, so that we can create new visions" (p. 12). hooks (1990) assures us that transgression can mean "pushing against oppressive boundaries set by race, sex, and class domination [as a form of] oppositional political struggle" (p. 145). Lashgari (1995) advises that "[t]o write honestly may mean transgressing, violating the literary boundaries of the expected and accepted" (p. 2).

hooks joins Lashgari as she positions herself on/in the margins in relation to the central, dominant position. This place is not to be thought of solely as a "site of deprivation . . . in fact [she] is saying just the opposite, that it is also a site of radical possibility, a space of resistance" (hooks, 1990, p. 149). The claiming of positions in the margins as spaces from which heteroglossia springs makes the dialogical process possible, and makes the margins central for feminist criticism. The margin is not a place one wishes to move away from, "to lose—to give up or surrender" (p. 149); rather, a marginal position is a chosen space "a site one stays in, clings to even, because it nourishes one's capacity to resist" (p. 150). Trinh T. Minh-ha (1991), likewise, claims the margins as "our sites of survival, [they] become our fighting grounds and . . . sites for pilgrimage" (p. 17).

A position on the margins gives teachers a unique viewpoint, as hooks (1990) says, a "radical perspective from which to see and create, to imagine alternatives, new worlds" (p. 150) with students. However, travesia can be disconcerting as we are challenged to not only engage the unknown ground of the "Other" but the "very ground under one's own feet" (Lashgari, 1995, p. 4). This can be particularly bewildering for those whose thinking has been developed by a monologic discourse.

Audre Lorde (1984) also claims her position on the margins as a position that gives her a particular and powerful vantage point. She indicates some of the costs as well as the delight in the community found in this position. Lorde encourages us to learn "how to stand alone, unpopular and sometimes reviled, and how to make common cause with those others identified as outside the structures in order to define and seek a world in which we can all flourish" (p. 112). Lorde assures us that the company we will find in our marginal experience, the community we will find, are those who have been defined as different by the dominant society. As Lorde says, "outside the circle of this society's definition of acceptable women . . . [are found] those of us who have been forged in the crucibles of difference" (Lorde, 1984, p. 112), including those who are "different" by virtue of economic status, race, sexual orientation, age, and so forth.

Silence into Voice

The metaphor of voice, or finding one's voice, has been a powerful and formative metaphor for my own work. "Voice" here does not refer to ordinary talk or everyday self-revelation. In its more radical sense it is the articulation of a perspective, an act of freedom and liberation. bell hooks expresses finding her own voice as a way of "talking back" and the "moving from silence into speech" (1989, p. 9). It is a way of moving from object to subject. Objects are voiceless, only spoken about, in that "our beings are defined and interpreted by others" (hooks, 1989, p. 12). Subjects are able to speak for themselves. "Talking back" then is the activity of "the oppressed, the colonized, the exploited, and those who stand and struggle side by side [as] a gesture of defiance that heals, that makes new life and new growth possible" (hooks, 1989, p. 9). Perhaps not so dramatic, yet every bit as brave was my student who was able to take a stand against the power of the prevailing discourse.

Adding one's voice to the dialogical process does have its costs, as Lashgari (1995) cautions. Lorde (1984) tells us that she has been afraid at times; she says, "of course I am afraid, because the transformation of silence into language and action . . . always seems fraught with danger" (p. 42). Even so, she shares with us a query regarding "what if she had been born mute or maintained an oath of silence" during her life for safety's sake. In the realization that pain and death are inescapable, she willingly accepts the scrutiny she has undergone by the particular way she has entered into "a process of life that is creative and continuing, that is growth" (p. 43). Therefore, there are risks to speaking out, to talking back, and yet we must realize that there are also risks in remaining silent.

These forms of feminist literary critique have had the expressed goal of talking back to a discourse that has sought to define and suppress counterdiscourses. Among the most deeply formative of my perspective is the work of Gloria Anzaldúa (1987). Through a series of autobiographical essays, for example, she speaks to attempts to "tame a wild tongue." She vividly depicts the attempts of her family, her church, her government, and her own struggle to overcome the "tradition of silence."

Anzaldúa (1987) refers to colonization in historical and metaphorical terms, and to the internalization of acceptable norms of the colonizers. Anzaldúa explains, "Dominant paradigms, predefined concepts that exist as unquestionable, unchallengeable, are transmitted to us by the culture. . . . [Many times] I heard mothers and mothers-in-law tell their sons to beat their wives for being *hociconas* (big mouths) . . . for expecting their husbands to help with the rearing of children " (p. 16).

More powerfully, her story is about resistance, a counterdiscourse that decenters and disorients a monologic perspective of the dominant society, laying bare its violence. Anzaldúa (1987) exposes a neocolonial propensity in current U.S. social and political discourse. For example, her works can address the conservative politics in the English-only movement in education: "Wild tongues can't be tamed, they can only be cut out" (p. 54). Anzaldúa's explanation of the connection of language and identity resists the assimilationist perspectives exemplified in the work of writers such as Richard Rodriquez (1983).

Critique of Science

"Heteroglossia" exists in science as well. Multiple counterdiscourses are found in the realm of the philosophy of science, for example. Sandra Harding (1991) has explained that there is a building skepticism about the "benefits that the sciences and their technologies can bring to society" (p. 1). Harding (1991) is forceful in noting that these feminist critiques "are not isolated voices crying in the wilderness . . . but are linked thematically and historically to a rising tide of critical analysis of the mental life and social relations of the modern, androcentric, imperial, bourgeois West, including its science and notions of knowledge" (p. viii).

Chris Weedon (1987) also explains that "within the official institutions of science and research, feminists have begun to challenge the boundaries of existing knowledge" (p. 14). Understandably, the critique comes from several positions since there are multiple, and often contradictory, feminist views.[1]

I want to make the point that the feminist perspective[2] that I espouse is not concerned with work that advances the cause of women only. On the contrary, feminism, as I relate to it, "encapsulates a distinctive value position, but these are truly human values, not just those of a 'women's perspective.' And so these values should be those of all people" (Stanley & Wise, 1993, p. 27). Feminists have joined this conversation not as a special interest group (Harding, 1991) who appeal a hearing for their benefit alone. Women join other feminists involved with other movements "as thinkers expressing concerns about science and society that are echoed in the other 'countercultures' of science—in antiracist and Third World movements, in anticapitalist movements, and in ecology and peace movements" (p. 50).

Finally, before moving into the three feminist models for critiquing science, I will discuss Harding's view of the oneness of the "hard" and "soft" sciences. Harding (1991) reminds us that an "influential tendency in conventional thought" (p. 15) is that there is actually one standard for all the sciences, or what counts as science, and that is the "hard" or natural sciences with physics ranking the highest. Social sciences are lower on the scale and many are considered "soft" depending on the extent to which their methodologies are less quantitative and more qualitative. Even so, psychology has a long-standing commitment to a positivist, empiricist epistemology and method. The influence of this commitment is "so pervasive as to be unrecognized by those enmeshed in its web of meaning, [as] it informs every aspect of psychology's undertakings" (Moke & Bohan, 1992, p. 7). This is no less true for educational psychology. Harding insists that the "sciences are fundamentally 'one,' and the model for that one is physics" (p. 15). Therefore, while some of the critiques offered below come out of the critiques of natural sciences, they have valid applications for the discipline of educational psychology as well.

What is needed, and what Harding (1991) attempts to do, is provide a counterdiscourse, a "critical examination of [science's] origins and values . . . to figure out just what are the regressive and the progressive tendencies brought into play in any particular scientific or feminist project, and how to advance the progressive and inhibit the regressive ones" (pp. 10–11).

Harding (1991) affirms the progressive themes in modern science that have yielded a high standard of living for many, "especially if we are white and middle or upper class" (p. 2). Harding also points to regressive themes that have yielded the atomic bombs, industrial exploitation of water, air, land, and, whole groups of people. To take the position that science contains both progressive and regressive tendencies is not to maintain that science is inherently good, bad, or "value-neutral" and used in only progressive and regressive ways. Harding (1991) takes a skeptical position regarding science; she acknowledges that this is "a confusing moment" (p. 2) in the relationship between science and feminism.

Harding (1996) takes as an additional focus, what she refers to as a "racial economy of science." She explains: "The institutions, assumptions, and practices that are responsible for disproportionately distributing along 'racial' lines the benefits of Western sciences to the haves, and the bad consequences to the have nots, thereby enlarging the gap between them" (p. 2).

Harding (1996) notes the problem in using the term *racial* in this way, realizing that issues of race cannot be separated from other issues of class and gender. She states that "there is no uncontroversial shorthand to use in referring to the complicity of Western sciences in projects of racism . . . colonialism . . . imperialism" (p. 20). "Elite" science educators are indicted as afflicted by a kind of scientific "illiteracy" through their failure to understand and teach others "systematic analyses of social origins, traditions, meanings, practices, institutions, technologies, uses and consequences" (p. 1) of the science they practice and teach.

Three Models of Critique

Harding's (1991) models frame the contemporary critique effectively. She acknowledges three models of critique of science, shifting from reform to revolution:

1. critique of bad science or feminist empiricism.
2. critique of science as a social problem, in and of itself.
3. critique of science-as-usual, including what she terms feminist standpoint epistemology.

The third model constitutes the most prevalent model of critique evident in the literature.

The first model of critique maintains the general belief in the positive value of science while taking the position that science needs to be reformed. This perspective critiques "bad science" (Harding, 1991). The critique is directed toward that science which results, for example, in bias or sexist conclusions. The critique is directed toward research in science that is flawed in that it does not "follow well-understood principles of method and theory" (Harding, 1991, p. 57). Those who associate with this perspective assume that an Archimedean vantage point is possible, and "support the goal of value-neutral objectivity and impartiality for all scientific inquiry" (p. 57). Harding refers to the feminist form of this conventional theory "as applied to science and its procedures for producing knowledge, [as] 'feminist empiricism'" (p. 58).

For example, Longino and Doell (1987) contend that it is possible to subvert sexist and androcentric bias in research programs through the use of "a variety of tactical responses" (p. 186) without denouncing science as an enterprise. They claim that the structure of science allows for the presentation of alternative accounts that are more ingenious and self-conscious.

Evelyn Fox Keller, historian of science, has been offered as an exemplar of this perspective (Haraway, 1991; Restivo, 1988). Keller is one who is interested in "correct[ing] the gender inequalities in modern science" (Restivo, 1988, p. 217) while remaining within the modern science paradigm.

There is another view of science that falls outside the reconstruction of a feminist science encouraged by Harding and others. Sal Restivo (1988), for example, argues that science itself is a social problem. Through his examination of the cultural roots of modern science he claims that modern science has been used as a "tool of the ruling elites . . . emerged and developed as an alienating and alienated mode of inquiry . . . [and these roots] are everywhere inseparable from military, political, and economic interests and power" (pp. 213–214).

Restivo argues that "purity" and "progress" are myths that serve only to enhance the power and privilege of modern science. What Restivo calls for is a "sociological imagination" developed by attention to new questions in the sociology of science. New questions, for example, may include: what do scientists produce and how do they produce it; what good are the products of science; in what social context is it valued and who values it; what are the goals, visions, and values of the work?

A sociological imagination is not an abstract exercise; rather, it is a call to action that challenges prevailing social arrangements. Restivo believes that something is missing from current critiques, including some feminist critiques, of science. He seeks a specific "blend of structural analysis, social criticism, epistemological relevance, and an activist orientation toward social change" (p. 208).

A third model, a critique of "science-as-usual," includes what Harding (1991) refers to as "feminist standpoint epistemology." This critique of science insists that no Archimedean perspective is possible because knowledge is socially situated, "grounded in particular, historical social situations" (Harding, 1991, p. 59). Views are always partial and distorted. Harding says, "I always see the world through my own culture's eyes; I think with its assumptions" (p. 59). Theorists from this perspective use as a resource "women's situation in a gender-stratified society" to show that research directed toward "social values and political agendas can nevertheless produce empirically and theoretically preferable results" (p. 119). This position is in contrast to the critique of "bad science" that, in the interest of objectivity, seeks to rid methodology of all subjectivity, including gender.

Harding makes particular comment that the unique perspective of feminist-standpoint epistemology is not connected to biological differences between men and women; rather, it is the unique position of women in a stratified society that gives a particular vantage point. Harding (1991) insists that this vantage point designates an "objective" location, i.e., women's lives "as the place from which feminist research should begin" (p. 123). This is considered a particularly trustworthy position as "members of oppressed groups have fewer interests in ignorance about the social order and few reasons to invest in maintaining or justifying the status quo than do dominant groups" (p. 126).

Collins (1990) offers that situated knowledge, like Black feminist thought, "is less likely than the specialized knowledge produced by dominant groups to deny the connection between ideas and the vested interest of their creators" (p. 234). Donna Haraway (1988) has also asserted a preference for the vantage point of members of subjugated groups saying, "there is good reason to believe vision [from this position] is better" (p. 583). It is not that there is something "innocent" about subjugated knowledges. Indeed, these also need to receive a critical examination and deconstruction. Rather, subjugated standpoints are preferred "because in principle they are least likely to allow denial of the critical and interpretive core of all knowledge" (Haraway, 1988, p. 581).

This model of critique is both an interrogation of "objectivity" and at the same time a call for a particular objectivity, which seems at first contradictory. Harding and others (e.g., Haraway, 1988; D. Smith, 1987) are calling for a program of "strong objectivity." This call comes out of a doubt that the scientific method is strong enough "to identify and eliminate distorting social interests and values" (Harding, 1996, p. 17) that intrude upon and distort the results of scientific research. What is needed is "causal analyses not just of the micro-processes in the laboratory but also the macro tendencies in the social order which shape scientific practices" (Harding 1991, p. 149). So, in other words, strong objectivity calls for a more determined focus on the values and beliefs that make scientific practice possible in the first place: "Women—and men—cannot understand or explain the world we live in or the real choices we have as long as the sciences describe and explain the world primarily from the perspectives of the lives of dominant groups" (Harding, 1991, p. 307).

Required here, along with strong objectivity, is the complementary process of a strong reflexivity whereby a researcher examines her own cultural beliefs and values through which she views the behaviors, values, and beliefs of those who are being studied. Harding (1991) explains that this strong reflexivity would require that "objects of inquiry be conceptualized as gazing back in all their cultural particularity" (p. 163); and, researchers, likewise "stand behind them, gazing back at his [sic] own socially situated research projects in all its cultural particularity" (p. 163).

Similarly, Haraway (1996) calls for a "critical" reflexivity as she acknowledges that "[n]othing comes without its world, so trying to know these worlds is crucial" (p. 440). She believes Harding's notion of strong reflexivity is akin to a concept she calls "diffraction," "to make different patterns in a more worldly way. . . . Diffraction patterns record the passage of difference, interaction, and interference" (Haraway, 1996, pp. 429–430).

Haraway instructs us that *tropes* are helpful in understanding diffraction. The etymological root of trope can be traced to the Greek *tropos:* "tropes [then] are what makes us swerve, what makes us notice what we did not already know how to see . . . a kind of aerobics for academics, perhaps" (p. 430).

This ability to "see" differently is emphasized by Haraway (1991) through the metaphor of "vision." She uses this metaphor in order to foreground the idea that the *gaze* of the scientist is embodied, always from somewhere, from within someone, even as it appears in mainstream scientific writing as a "gaze from nowhere . . . [that claims] the power to see and not be seen, to represent while escaping representation" (p. 188). The "eye" of the one who is looking has a growing capacity to see because of "visualizing technologies." Through these technologies, vision can be "endlessly enhanced . . . [until] all perspective gives way to an infinitely mobile vision, which no longer seems just mythically about the god-trick of seeing everything from nowhere, but to have put the myth into ordinary practice" (p. 189). This idea will be more fully discussed in chapter 5.

The ability to see endlessly from nowhere is an illusion, of course. What Haraway wants to emphasize is the potency of the vision science claims to have. Contrastingly, it is the recognition that our "only partial perspective promises objective vision" (p. 190). The "objectivity" that is possible from our particular and partial perspective is about a "limited location and situated knowledge, not about transcendence . . . [or] omniscience" (Haraway, 1991, p. 190).

What is at issue in this aspect of feminist critique of science is more than concerns regarding particular theories, the scientific method, scientific technologies, and the institutions in which they are constructed. Harding (1991) wants to clarify how deeply we, i.e., "those most at home in Western societies" (p. 3), are embedded in a Western, scientific worldview, so much so that it is difficult to see how scientific rationality has infiltrated our belief systems and our epistemologies. At the same time it is important to realize that "the social origins of science and the values it carries suffuse scientific projects . . . what science becomes in any historical era depends on what we make of it" (p. 10).

Thus, feminist critique of science-as-usual brings the study of scientific research to a very different site of investigation as the perspective is concerned with the process of science itself. Steve Woolgar (1988) remarks that it is "only comparatively recently that critical attention has been directed towards the 'internal' workings of science" (p. 9). Although various disciplines have challenged conventional views of science "the practice of science is itself the object of critical scrutiny" (p. 9). Several members within the science community have taken up the interrogation of scientific discourse in a way that exposes a remarkable social dynamic and political agenda of the discourse. It is a real "heteroglossia." Where traditionally there was thought to be only objectivity, neutrality, truth, and progress, following from Harding's (1991) model of a critique of science-as-usual there now is appreciation for the social and political dynamics at work in these discourses. This concern for the internal workings of science, especially as it is expressed through scientific discourse, is central to my project as I believe it exposes some of science's regressive proclivities.

A few examples of work exemplifying this critique of science-as-usual may be helpful: Ruth Hubbard (1989) is concerned with the "context-stripping" methodology of science whereby the scientist is invisible and the results are represented as objective, value-neutral, and apolitical. Hubbard explains that "the context-stripping that worked reasonably well for the classical physics of falling bodies has become the model for how to do every kind of science" (p. 127), even given the insight of Heisenberg's uncertainty principle.[3] "Science is a social process" (p. 119), Hubbard insists, and "generating facts is a social enterprise" (p. 119). Nevertheless, even the language of science reinforces the illusion of facts rendered in a vacuum as it "implicitly denies the relevance of time, place, social context, authorship, and personal responsibility" (p. 125).

Hubbard (1989) is also concerned with the homogeneity of those who do science (i.e., Western European, North American, middle/upper-class males) as "public accountability is not built into the system" (p. 121). She points out that "small groups of people with similar personal and academic backgrounds" (p. 120) decide who gets to be faculty, whose work gets funded, who gets published, i.e., who gets rewarded by the system. She complains that "science is made . . . by the chosen for the chosen" (p. 120). In Hubbard and Wald (1993) the focus remains on these social and political implications through a description of work performed with DNA. Hubbard and Wald's aim in writing their book is to demystify some of the language and concepts of genetics and biotechnology as they believe that it is "crucial that we, as citizens, not leave this process in the hands of 'experts.' Like other people, scientists are interested in seeing their projects flourish, and their enthusiasm can blind them to the possible negative effects of their work" (p. xiii).

Hubbard (1989) highlights the political content of science and its governing role. She maintains that "Science and technology always operate in somebody's interest and serve someone or some group of people" (p. 128). Hubbard asserts that "[t]o the extent that scientists are 'neutral' that merely means that they support the existing distribution of interests and power" (p. 128).

Elizabeth Fee puts this another way by characterizing "objectivity" as "merely a code word for the political passivity of those scientists who have tacitly agreed to accept a privileged social position and freedom of inquiry within the laboratory in return for their silence in not questioning the social uses of science or the power relations that determine its direction" (Fee, quoted in Harding, 1987, p. 337).

Marion Namenwirth (1986), coming from the perspective of the biological sciences challenges her readers to make personal assessments of "whether the science we practice today has not strayed unacceptably far from the science of which we would like to take part" (p. 18). She critiques the presumption that scientists are able to remove themselves and their work from cultural and political influences. By "cloaking" their scientific projects in "claims of neutrality, detachment, and objectivity, scientists augment the perceived importance of their views, absolve themselves of social responsibility for the applications of their work, and leave their (unconscious) minds wide open to political and cultural assumptions" (p. 29). Namenwirth wants to make the point that being unconscious of the bias or the political agenda of work does not render the work neutral or objective. Rather, these "hidden influences and biases are particularly insidious in science because the cultural heritage of the practitioners is so uniform as to make these influences difficult to detect and unlikely to be brought to light" (p. 29).

The metaphor of "cloaking" scientific activity in neutrality and objectivity so as to cover particular political and social underpinnings of science is explicitly stated in the work of Ruth Bleier (1986). Bleier uses the image of "lab coat" to make her point that this covering of the scientist and the scientific activity denotes a kind of "innocence—of a pristine and aseptic neutrality—and gives him . . . a faceless authority that his audience can't challenge" (p. 67). Bleier's means to connect this cloaked or coated figure with that of the "Klansman," another faceless authority. Bleier does not shrink from this comparison; rather she emphasizes that she considers her work in science as a disruption and a subversion to misogynist, racist, regressive tendencies in science.

Many feminist scholars critique science from the point of male domination (e.g., Keller, 1986; Sherif, 1987; Whatley, 1986). Reasons for this domination have been located in the "deep-seated dualisms of Western culture [which] have encouraged and maintained a hierarchical domination (Harding & O'Barr, 1987, p. 33). The notion of hierarchical dualisms was articulated in ancient Greek and Egyptian philosophies. Human persons become fragmented through the view that "reality is segmented into spirit and matter" (Speight, Myers, Cox, & Highlen, 1991, p. 31). *Spirit* is a "transcendent principle" and is connected with activity, autonomy, reason, the mind, the permanent, and the infinite. In contrast, *matter* is the principle signifying immanence that "shows itself in passivity, dependence, emotions, the body, the physical, nature, the transitory, the finite" (Johnson, 1993, p. 11). In the original framework these two, matter and spirit, existed in a "harmonious tension of opposites" (p. 11) that gradually was separated, graded, and eventually became portrayed as polar opposites in which the differences were maximized. Thus, one became valued over the other; spirit is valued over matter in Western epistemologies.

Spirit is frequently connected with the rational mind,[4] the intellect, and the masculine, while matter is connected to the earth, the body, and the feminine. The effect was a hierarchy of mind over body, male over female. These dualisms are social constructions, and like so many dualisms in science, and psychology in particular, are not neutral constructions; rather, they have political implications, they affect power relationships. Such dualisms sanctioned women being kept out of institutions of higher learning and out of science laboratories. When they were able to surmount barriers placed in their way their work and their contributions were often trivialized and/or marginalized.[5]

One of the most widely used dualisms in psychology is "nature vs. nurture." The distinction has been around for centuries originally expressed as "nature vs. culture" and expressed formally over one hundred years ago by Galton who introduced the dualism while concerned with the heritability of "intelligence" that he was trying to measure. Historically, nature-nurture "has been used almost without exception, as a weapon to diminish the importance of groups derogated by the culture—Blacks, Irish, Jews, women, gays, the handicapped, among them" (Kessen, 1993, p. 271). Restivo (1988) explains that the "dichotomy between 'nature' and 'culture' . . . has fostered a dominative, exploitative orientation to nature, women, workers, and the underclass in general" (p. 219). This dualism, taken as a commonsense notion in current educational psychology discourse, has been criticized as it "divides what cannot be divided and it contrasts what cannot be contrasted" (Kessen, 1993, p. 271).

Many of the counterdiscourses offered by the feminist scholarship reported in this chapter are challenging current social arrangements. Their narrative "reveals and invents disruptive images of what could be" (Fine, 1992, p. 221). This work presents a counterdiscourse to the discipline of educational psychology so embedded in mainstream science. Like so much feminist criticism, it highlights the social, cultural, and political implications of positionality as it constructs what can be said and seen, what remains silenced and hidden in the discipline's discourse.

Research within traditional paradigms will not allow the kind of talking back that is called for by feminist critique. New research paradigms are required. This is the discussion of the following chapter.

CHAPTER 3

Critical Educational Research

This chapter has a dual purpose. First, I am employing a research approach that is "critical." I want to emphasize how this approach is different from traditional methodologies employed in educational research and in educational psychology in particular. By "methodology" I am referring to the "intellectual means" that focuses my research project (Stanley & Wise, 1993). Second, I will describe the strategies of analysis that will be utilized with this particular methodology, i.e., critical discourse analysis, in the following chapters of this book.

There is a growing debate regarding every aspect of educational research within the educational community. For example, Maxine Greene (1994) describes what she calls a "restiveness" that accompanies a rising skepticism regarding contemporary educational research. This uneasiness stems from interrogations regarding the "normal course of science" and "the best scientific research." Greene insists this situation has resulted in "a growing disenchantment with technicism and bland objectivist assumptions . . . separation of research or positive inquiry from moral considerations or ethical perplexities . . . [as well as] the apparent uselessness of research in overcoming "savage inequalities" (Greene, 1994, p. 424). Greene purports that while many researchers do not question the uses of science, there are increasing numbers of researchers whose work flows from an uneasiness that is, in fact, a kind of rebellion against mainstream science. Educationalists are encouraged to consider "a number of fresh perspectives" (Greene, 1994, p. 426) that reject "[p]ositivistic and depersonalized approaches to science" (p. 437). Thus, Greene reports a shift in research practice.

This state of educational research that troubles many educators is beyond the frequent quantitative/qualitative debate (e.g., Eisner, 1992; Maxwell, 1992; Peshkin, 1993; Popkewitz, 1992; Schrag, 1992; J. K. Smith, 1983). Much of the dissatisfaction with current educational research is connected to the current social and political milieu that has been referred to as a "conservative restoration" (Apple, 1993, 1996). It is argued that the discourse of education is dominated by conservative tendencies regarding questions of "what education is for, what and whose knowledge is considered legitimate, and who has the right to answer these questions" (Apple, 1996, p. 9).

Greene (1994) articulates a challenge for educational research that, while not completely replacing work done within the mainstream scientific model, interrogates its methods and its results, and creates a space where emancipatory projects may be explicated. She tells us that what has become "crucial in the contemporary conversation is the contingency of language, along with the notion that truth is made rather than found" (p. 444). Greene desires that educators join together in a struggle "to go in search of those intersections where deficiencies exist, where there are calls for justice, where freedom is being awaited" (p. 459). Greene (1994) expresses a profound sense of hope for more meaningful and transformative kinds of educational research. Greene is recognizing the potential that a "critical" approach has to offer social science research. It is this critical approach to educational research that I take up in this work.

Employing a critical approach indicates a significant shift away from the conventional models of research; it has little to do with educational researchers utilizing positivist or interpretivist conceptual and methodological paradigms. This shift deserves at least a brief explanation because it is helpful in locating work done within a critical perspective. I will briefly explain how both the positivist (or quantitative) and interpretivist (or qualitative) approaches are connected to the project of modernity, and why these perspectives are unsuitable for many critical research interests. I propose an explanation regarding why a critical, poststructuralist perspective is more appropriate, and what this approach has to offer the contemporary research scene.

Educational Research and the Project of Modernity

Modernity's[1] project was to discover and deliver the "truth" about the world. Modernity developed as a response to a premodern worldview in which meaning and order, emanating from nature and God, was mediated to society through voices of authority in the person of the sovereign and/or the religious leader. Modernity offered the promise of releasing people from "the bonds of ignorance associated with stagnant traditions, narrow religions, and meager educations" (Bloland, 1995, p. 2). Modernity was committed to the liberation of "the world from the chains of superstition, ignorance, and suffering" (Giroux, 1983a, p. 11).

Modernity's aim was to replace premodern fantasy, faith, and superstition with scientific knowledge. Usher and Edwards (1994) remind us: "Science becomes the guarantor and route to truth and emancipation. The emancipation of humanity thus requires that people are given access to scientific knowledge, since the condition of their emancipation is that they live subject to the 'laws' uncovered by science" (p. 172). This emancipation would occur as "reason" became "deified" (Kincheloe, 1993) as *the* authority. Reason was hailed as the "source of progress in knowledge and society, as well as the privileged locus of truth and the foundation of systematic knowledge" (Best & Kellner, 1991, p. 2). For some philosophers, modernity marks the beginning "of a developmental process resulting from technological progress, liberated needs and the triumph of the Spirit. . . . [which makes] science, rather than God, central to society" (Touraine, 1995, p. 9). Modernity has been identified "with the belief in linear progress, absolute truths, the rational planning of ideal social orders, and the standardization of knowledge and production" (Sarup, 1996, p. 94). Order is established through the discovery of universal, impersonal laws. Order is important because chaos seems to be the only alternative to order from within this meaning-making system (Bauman, 1991).

Positivist Educational Research

Positivism[2] is the modernist method, logic, and pathway to truth and order (Slife & Williams, 1997). This mode of educational research enjoys a privileged position among other epistemologies (Fenstermacher, 1994). Educational research has long been conceptualized as primarily a positivistic undertaking (Schrag, 1992) that appropriates the concepts and methodologies of the natural sciences to arrive at knowledge. Giroux (1981) refers to the "positivist culture" in which educational research is embedded. When social sciences adopt this positivist perspective there are two implicit assumptions (Carr & Kemmis, 1986). The first assumption concerns the consideration of the aims, concepts, and methods employed by the natural sciences as appropriate to social science questions. The second assumption understands that the natural science model of explanation "provides the logical standards by which the explanations of the social sciences can be assessed" (Carr & Kemmis, 1986, p. 62).

Educational research from a positivist perspective exemplifies distinct characteristics. For instance, in a positivist perspective there is a confidence in a particular methodology following from a specific epistemological orientation. A positivist perspective also maintains certain assumptions about language. There exists a particular relationship between researcher and researched as well as theory and practice. These will be discussed briefly.

Method, i.e., the *hypothetico-deductive* scientific method, is of critical importance because it is understood as the way to access an "accurate reflection or measurement of an independently existing object" (J. K. Smith, 1983, p. 9). Method is a pivotal aspect of any scientific undertaking as fidelity to a series of procedures from within an established program ensures the "journey to the facts" (J. K. Smith, 1983, p. 10). To the degree that the methodology is "sound" and allows for a neutral, objective investigation of the variables under examination the results can be trusted.

The source of knowledge, from a positivist perspective, is events in the real world. Knowledge and truth are based on a correspondence supposition, i.e., what is true is what corresponds to reality. Science is purported to be able to yield pure and objective knowledge, a mirror image, about this world (Gergen, 1985; J. K. Smith, 1983) through empirical investigations.

Concepts under study are considered existing a priori in the real world, apart and distinct from the researcher, and regardless of researcher interest. There is an accepted view of language used to refer to and describe these concepts that is utilitarian. In this view, words are "implicitly assumed to function as simple transmitters of information from the writer to the reader. . . . [Words are a] somewhat unimportant container for information about phenomena, data, and theories" (Madigan et al., 1995, pp. 433–434). Therefore, the meanings of the words that are used are considered transparent, unambiguous, and fixed (Popkewitz, 1992).

The definition of concepts is determined within the rules and relationships of the particular discourse community that uses them. Gage and Berliner (1991), for example, illustrate this approach in referring to the development of the concept of "intelligence" within the educational psychology community:

> A concept is the organized information *we have* (emphasis added) about an entity. . . . The meaning, boundaries, and relationships connected with a concept are derived from everything *we know* (emphasis added) about that concept. . . . What *we mean* (emphasis added) by a concept is partly a matter of definition and partly a matter of the methods of studying the concept. . . . for example, the meaning of the concept of intelligence depends in part on how *we define* (emphasis added) *intelligence* (emphasis in original). (pp. 12–13)

It is this understanding that allows Herrnstein and Murray (1994) in their controversial book, *The Bell Curve,* to make the statement: "the word *intelligence* (emphasis in original) describes something real" (p. 1). This power to define abstract concepts as actual entities is a very central function of positivist science in its construction of order.

Abstract concepts considered to have "real" material existence points to the linguistic problem of reification (Gergen, 1985). This is a common occurrence within a positivist framework. Abstract constructs are used as "variables" in empirical investigations. As J. K. Smith (1983) points out: "Because the subjects studied in educational research, such as aptitude and motivation, admittedly do not have a material existence, how can it be implied that they are like physical objects. . . . What is important is not the nature of the objects, but how they are treated . . ." (p. 9). It is the treatment of these terms which is important, i.e., abstract concepts are treated *as though* they exist.

The position of the researcher is a significant characteristic of this perspective as "the persona of the writer [assumes] a low profile in the text" (Madigan et al., 1995, p. 433). The researcher is presented as detached from the object under study and insignificant, almost receding into the background as the importance of the data takes center stage. This allows the focus to remain on the object of the study, increasing the possibility of "creating the impression of neutrality or impersonal detachment . . . that is generally characteristic of the empirical disciplines" (Madigan et al., 1995, p. 433). The language of the scientific method itself gives the "impression of . . . impersonal detachment [of the researcher]. . . . keeping the focus on the phenomena under study" (Madigan et al., 1995, p. 431). The assumption is that "the facts speak for themselves."

Finally, the relationship of theory and practice has a pivotal position within this viewpoint. Educationalists espousing a positivist perspective assume that the schooling process is enhanced and improved to the extent that teachers utilized the knowledge accessed through the scientific method. Practice based on scientific principles and laws are believed to be able to offer certainty and rational solutions to educational questions that are understood as "technical" in nature. Popkewitz (1992) explains that this view puts the "researcher in the position of doing the enhancing and producing the progress, and defining the individuals who would be affected" (p. 14). This particular, one-way account (Carr & Kemmis, 1986) of the relation of theory and practice indicates a metaphor of researcher as "social engineer" (Carr & Kemmis, 1986; J. K. Smith, 1983).

Educational psychology has espoused a positivistic perspective from the beginning of its becoming formalized as a discipline. In the early part of this century Edward L. Thorndike contended that "[t]he profession of teaching will improve in proportion as its members direct their daily work by the scientific method" (Quoted in Carr & Kemmis 1986, p. 56). It is important to note that this movement toward a more science-based practice was simultaneously a movement away from a more traditional philosophical perspective. Professional schools began to aspire to a more prestigious position within the university. Teacher education as a field sought higher status by positioning itself as closely as possible to "the rigor of science-based knowledge" (Schon, 1987, p. 9). The belief followed that as teachers utilized an educational theory based on the methodology of the natural sciences, their practice would take on a "more rational basis. . . . purged of its metaphysical, ideological and normative elements" (Carr & Kemmis, p. 62).

This is a particular irony in this situation. As education became an increasingly "professionalized" field, educators believed that interference by "outsiders" would be minimized through the use of the increasingly prestigious scientific method. It seems paradoxical that "science," once considered the means of "democratizing knowledge" (Gordon, Miller, & Rollock, 1990) in response to the control of the political and religious aristocracy of premodern times, would itself become a means of elite control of knowledge through its positivist epistemology and technical language. This situation has been referred to as the "paradox of the scientific method" (Gordon et al., 1990) in that "rationalism, positivism, and logical empiricism represent major advances in humans' pursuit of knowledge and understanding. . . . [and at the same time] carries [sic] the potential for tyranny" (p. 15). Gergen (1994) notes the irony as well in that " 'science talk' [has become] as totalizing as that of the demagogy that science has sought to replace" (p. 413). This "science talk" pervades all aspects of our lives and claims "its own monopoly on the truth" (Rosenau, 1992, p. 9).

The confidence in the relationship between positivist science and teaching is clearly evidenced in the contemporary educational scene (Berliner & Rosenshine, 1987; Gage, 1985; Gage & Berliner, 1991; Woolfolk, 1995). Even so, it certainly is not the only type of knowledge utilized in teaching. Fenstermacher (1994) notes the "radically disjunctive conceptions of science" (p. 35) that are coming to the fore, including the practical knowledge of teachers themselves. Nevertheless, the resilience of the positivist paradigm is obvious today despite attacks leveled against it (Schrag, 1992). Although this epistemological perspective with its approach to research is pervasive and robust, it is also vulnerable on several counts, some of which are discussed below.

Interpretivist Educational Research

Quantitative methods and positivist epistemology proved unsatisfactory and/or inadequate for addressing particular educational questions and issues. Therefore, alternative research methodologies began to be recognized and explored. New epistemologies were acknowledged and appropriate methods sought. The most popular approach, described as a kind of countermovement (J. K. Smith, 1983), is characterized as an interpretive model utilizing qualitative methods.

The positivist perspective views society, or the teaching-learning situation in education, as "an 'independent system' maintained through the relationship of factors external to its members" (Carr & Kemmis, 1986, p. 84). In contrast, educational researchers who espouse an interpretivist or qualitative perspective view social reality as possessing an "intrinsic meaning structure" (Carr & Kemmis, 1986) generated by social actors. Hence the term *new sociology* is often used to describe this perspective. The aim of research is not empirical generalizations, the production of law-like statements, nor the establishment of functional relationships (van Manen, 1990). Rather, what is sought is understanding and meaning of situations, i.e., *Verstehen*. Through a deeper understanding of the situation the social actor is able to work more "thoughtfully and tactfully" (van Manen, 1990). When social actions are understood more deeply, when the significance of the actions are "enlightened or illuminated," practical change is possible (Carr & Kemmis, 1986). This signifies a dynamic relationship between theory and practice. Carr & Kemmis (1986) express this dynamic cogently: "The account of the theory-practice relationship of interpretive social science is thus two-way traffic of ideas into action; of practice from theoretical principles. The traffic is two way: practical deliberation is informed not only by ideas but also by the practical exigencies of situations; it also requires critical appraisal and mediation by the judgment of the actor" (p. 93).

The focus of this approach in educational research is on "understanding" the dynamic nature of the culture of the school organization or the classroom, rather than "discovering" an a priori "objective" form of knowledge of the positivist viewpoint.

The interpretivist perspective finds its source in a distinct epistemological orientation just as the positivist view espouses a particular model of knowledge. Gergen (1985) refers to the interpretivist model as the "endogenic" model of the "origins of knowledge. . . . [and] depends on processes (sometimes viewed as innate) endemic to the organism" (Gergen, 1985, p. 269). Humans strive to make sense of their world cognitively, and meaning is negotiated and renegotiated (Giroux, 1983b) in social situations. The focus has shifted from an impersonal objectivity, an "exogenic" model (Gergen, 1985), toward a deeper understanding of the notion that "through the use of language and thought human beings constantly produce meanings as well as interpret the world in which they find themselves" (Giroux, 1983, p. 184). "Objectivity" and "reality" are designated by the social actors themselves "in the process of interpreting their social world, [as they] externalize and objectify it" (Carr & Kemmis, 1986, p. 84).

Qualitative research continues to be committed to the pursuit of "objective knowledge" in that the "investigator claims to achieve an accurate representation of the world" (Gergen, 1985, p. 269). Researchers continue to assume the role of generally detached observers, investigators, and objective descriptors of the group or activity being researched. The results are thought to be reflections or representations of what is really there (Stanley & Wise, 1993). Thus, this research paradigm comfortably finds a place in the project of modernity along with the positivist paradigm because modernity is "characterized by a hermeneutic search for an underlying and unified truth and certainty that can render the world, experiences and events . . . coherent and meaningful" (Usher & Edwards, 1994, p. 12).

There are several criticisms of this interpretivist approach. One line of critique comes from the positivist orientation asserting that this approach is unable to make generalizations or "to provide 'objective' standards for verifying or refuting theoretical accounts" (Carr & Kemmis, 1986, p. 94). Another line of criticism asserts that "the core of the new sociology lacks an adequate theory of social change and consciousness" (Giroux, 1988, p. 25). The focus remains at the micro-level of the school or classroom, and the social and political structures, which influence what is understood and regarded as "knowledge" and meaning, are never exposed. Knowledge is "treated as a specific social act with its underlying social relationships" (Giroux, 1983a, p. 185). However, this epistemology is particularly problematic as it never moves beyond a relativistic view of knowledge. The negotiated meanings of social actors do affect the social structure, yet there is no consideration given to how the social structure impacts and constrains the meaning systems of the actors (Carr & Kemmis, 1986; Giroux, 1983b, 1988).

The qualitative approach is gaining popularity in educational research particularly with the rise of ethnographic studies. However, it is not likely to gain prevalence in educational research. This may be because the positivist perspective "forms the metatheoretical basis of science itself" (Gergen, 1985, p. 269).

A Critical Research Perspective

A critical approach to educational research takes the position that both the positivist and the interpretivist models are inadequate in their view of educational practice and attempts at reform that follow from this research. The positivist aim of technical prediction and control, and the interpretivist aim of practical understanding can never lead to the kind of reform and transformation that is necessary to ameliorate the injustice that provokes the current educational crisis. What is needed is a way of looking at education and educational research that allows questioning beyond the search for objective certitudes. The postmodern critique holds such a possibility.

Postmodern Critique

I am using the term *postmodernism*[3] in the sense of critique, a kind of "oppositional attitude" as employed by Foucault (Usher & Edwards, 1994). It is a way of looking at modernity's master narratives of science with their promise and project of progress, universality, and neutrality of scientific method and knowledge claims (Usher & Edwards, 1994). Postmodernist critique rejects the notion that scientific theory can ever mirror nature; at best it is a "partial perspective" (Best & Kellner, 1991). Its "knowledge claims are themselves partial, local, and specific rather than universal and ahistorical" (Usher & Edwards, 1994, p. 10).

Just as the "authority" in premodern times held by the priest and king was displaced by reason's claim to truth and certainty in modernity, postmodern critique and analysis interrupts power relationships that have been so effective in establishing the "truth" of the social sciences in the modern epoch.[4] This rejection of the scientific discourse is a confrontation with authority.

The scientific activity of modernity has shown itself vulnerable to criticism. The "truth" of modernism is a "thing of this world" (Foucault, 1980a, p. 131) since it is made in history and culture; knowledge considered as truth is the result of a social activity (Gergen, 1985). That "science" does not recognize itself as a human project is its major flaw (Rosenau, 1992; Usher & Edwards, 1994). Scholars writing about science claim that its truth can be somehow separate and distant, objective, and not "encumbered" with values and ideologies. A common metaphor for these assertions is the idea that language can be wrapped in the "cloak" of objectivity and neutrality (Bleier, 1986; Namenwirth, 1986; Usher & Edwards, 1994). Thus, postmodern analysis is a critique of the claim of modern scientific research that it is possible to the world "in a direct and unmediated way—as it really is" (Usher & Edwards, 1994, p. 19).

As the positivistic and interpretivistic research paradigms have a particular epistemological stance, so does a critical approach. Social constructionism[5] (Gergen, 1983, 1985) challenges the concept of knowledge as mental representation. Knowledge, including scientific knowledge, is a social construction (Scarr, 1985). In other words, knowledge is what passes for knowledge, the result of "negotiated intelligibility" (Gergen, 1985). The locus of human knowing shifts from the "interior regions of the mind [to the] processes and structures of human interaction" (Gergen, 1985, p. 271). Gergen (1995) stresses the "negotiated" aspect of understanding. This negotiated understanding takes place among "complex networks of writers and readers [who comprise a] discourse community" (Madigan et al., 1995, p. 429), supporters of a particular paradigm (Kuhn, 1970), or "epistemic community" (Usher & Edwards, 1994). The members of these groups share a distinctive worldview, set of beliefs, and language.

Seen from this perspective, then, the "grand narratives of science, truth, and progress are discourses—'realities' we have created by and for ourselves. Stories we tell ourselves about the real or, more likely, stories told by 'powerful' others on our behalf" (Usher & Edwards, 1994, p. 28). Critical postmodern traditions recognize the political underpinnings of knowledge production. Those concerned with this line of research engage in visioning and re-visioning relations of power within the society (Popkewitz, 1995) so as to be able to move toward action. Giroux (1988) explains: "Inherent in this [critical] perspective is an intersection of theory, ideology, and social practice. . . . The cutting edge of this perspective is its insistence on connecting macro forces in the larger society to micro analysis such as classroom studies" (p. 27). For example, a critical analysis of the discourse of educational psychology is aimed at understanding and explicating how the discourse of this discipline, while considered a particular discourse community's expression of the "truth," is implicated in a larger struggle between dominant and subordinate discourses (Aronowitz & Giroux, 1991). Even the specialized and technical texts of educational psychology are part of larger social texts (Scholes, 1985). These texts need to be understood and read within these con-texts.

Critical research in the social sciences is a political activity and value-laden work. Research within this critical perspective takes as its aim not the furthering of the discipline's discourse, but rather, the aim is to make assumptions of educational psychology explicit in order to subvert their claims (Rosenau, 1992). The claims of the discipline must be subverted as they serve to give some groups in the society unfair advantage and disadvantage to other groups (J. Thomas, 1993).

This position of the researcher has been challenged. Many feminist and critical researchers (see chapter 2) criticize the stance that separates the observer from the observed in the interest of "objectivity." Michelle Fine (1992) contends that this detached stance neglects "to discuss why one research question or interpretation prevailed over others . . . [this stance renders] oblique the ways in which we, as researchers, construct our analysis and narratives" (p. 211). Fine (1992) warns feminist researchers that if we do not take "critical, activist, and open stances on our own work, then we collude in reproducing social silences through the social sciences" (p. 206). Josselson and Lieblich (1996) assert the importance of "allowing people to tell the real story of their work—to consider their own role" (p. 651) in their research projects.

A critical perspective recognizes that any viewpoint is partial and incomplete. Partiality is accepted as a way I come to realize my view, and the view of others, as *embodied,* rather than distanced. I am conscious of a particular, shifting, location as I do this work; I have no desire to dislocate myself from it. In other words, I have no interest in doing research about the world from a position apart from the world. Recognizing the influence of a situated view makes no promise of seeing in a neutral and objective way or of "transcendence of all limits and responsibility" (Haraway, 1991) as is implied through the impersonal detachment of the positivist epistemology.

Appreciation of the partial view of the researcher tends toward the possibility of community.[6] Rosaldo (1993) explains this notion: "Each viewpoint is arguably incomplete—a mix of insight and blindness, reach and limitations, neither omniscience nor a unified master narrative but complex understandings of ever-changing, multifaceted social realities" (p. 128). This multiplicity of viewpoints and voices has an important place in educational research within a democratic society.

Critical Discourse Analysis and Educational Psychology

Three points will be addressed in this section: first, the arrival of critical discourse analysis (CDA) on the educational research scene; second, the relevancy of critical discourse analysis; third, the salience of language within this research perspective.

Critical discourse analysis has had a relatively recent arrival onto the educational research scene and has been described as a "new wave" of research (Burman & Parker, 1993). It has been noted that before the 1980s "educational researchers would have been hard pressed to turn up many theses, research papers, and monographs that used discourse-analytic theories and methods" (Luke, 1995, p. 7). However, the fact that CDA is gaining legitimacy is evidenced in the 1995–1996 edition of *Review of Research in Education* (Apple, 1995) in which it is reviewed in the first chapter. Apple states that the purpose of the editorial board of this publication is to "give a greater voice to 'newer' forms of research methodologies and theories" (p. xi); the editors want to encourage readers to "think socially" (p. xiii).

The research reviewed in this yearbook has a common purpose, i.e., to place educational institutions in context, to make clear the importance of recognizing that "[e]ducational institutions do not stand alone, somehow distanced from the cultural, economic, and political relations and tensions of the larger society" (p. xii). Issues regarding education, the institutions, practices, and discourses that education employs, need to be viewed as part of a more general, social, and complex problematic. The section of the book on CDA, for example, expresses a deep concern regarding "the connections between discourse and power in education . . . [and the implications with] the cultural and socioeconomic transformations now going on in the larger society" (p. xvi).

Critical discourse analysis is particularly relevant during these times of educational "crisis" and "reform." Luke (1995) cites two demographic and socioeconomic transformations that have emphasized the need for CDA as issues of language, discourse, and difference have taken center stage on the educational agenda.

One transformation is the recognition of educational entitle-
ments, the "enfranchisement of cultural and linguistic minori-
ties into mainstream public discourses and institutions" (p. 4).
Failure to address this issue and the concomitant sociocultural
changes and conflicts "could pose serious limitations in the capacity of educators to address what remains a political issue of
access and equity" (p. 5).

The second transformation is connected to the shift from an industrialized to a service-based and information-based economy
(Luke, 1995; Usher & Edwards, 1994) that has given rise to "new
forms of language and information based work" (Luke, 1995, p. 5).
In this environment spoken and written language is "the principal medium of commercial exchange. Texts, images, and representations have become both the means and objects of processes
of commodification" (p. 5). It is within this context that issues of
representation and subjectivity are of paramount importance as
schools are called upon to ensure access and equity to an increasingly diverse student population. Luke (1995) emphasizes that
"different kinds of children are, in turn, affiliated with differing
kinds of power and capital in discourse communities and economic institutions" (p. 38). In this "educational context . . . the
tensions between official discourses and minority discourses
should be principle focuses for educational research" (p. 38).

The salience of language is increasingly recognized in research,
particularly within various approaches to discourse analysis.
Luke (1995) explains three methods frequently used in educational research: psycholinguistic, sociolinguistic, and poststructuralist analysis. Psycholinguistics understands the creative, developing child as a "language user" whose growing competence
accounts for the complexity of language development. Sociolin-
guistics takes as its focus the social nature of language and language development as connected to socialization. The third approach, and the approach that impacts the work here, is
concerned with a poststructuralist analysis where the constructing character of language is central. The constructing dynamic of
language is discussed below.

"Method" in Critical Discourse Analysis

There is a need to be clear when talking about critical discourse
analysis in terms of "method." The category of method "comes

from a discourse developed for quantitative, positivist mythologies such as experiments and surveys" (Wetherell & Potter, 1992, p. 101). Within the positivist framework "sound" methodology leads to a degree of "authority" with which outcomes of the research seem justified. Gergen (1985) insists that the "sciences have been enchanted by the myth that the assiduous application of rigorous method will yield sound fact" (p. 273). No such confidence in "method" exists in a critical research paradigm.

Discourse analysis is more of a craft skill, and therefore its method is not easily described in an explicit, step-by-step manner. As a person's skills increase at the craft and it is explained exactly what discrete procedures are used, the task becomes more complex. Although there are specific "analytic considerations," the accent is on the craft, developing a skill, cultivating a "more conscious and theorized understanding of how to be a cultural member" (Wetherell & Potter, 1992, p. 104). The focus of CDA is clearly on becoming a better craftsperson, or a cultural worker in Giroux's sense, rather than performing a particular set of mechanical procedures.

In short, there is not a set mechanics for "doing" critical discourse analysis, and this is problematic as it may appear "as an improvisation . . . [I]ndeed, from a functionalist point of view it hardly appears to be a methodology at all" (Gottlieb, 1987, p. 276). Critical discourse analysts view their work "as an art achieved through practice. There is no determinate method . . . in the sense of explicit rules that are to be followed" (Bernstein quoted in Gottlieb, 1987, p. 278). Critical discourse analysis is a way of looking at things and articulating a type of "heteroglossic expression" that brings into play "various discursive resources with which to read, interpret, and make sense" (Luke, 1995, p. 39).

Discourse

From a positivist-empiricist perspective discourse might be interpreted as referring "to what is said and written and passes for more or less orderly thought and exchange of ideas" (Cherryholmes, 1988, p. 2). In general, discourse means the text and the talk (van Dijk, 1993b) of a particular community.

Even so, discourses do not simply express or reflect ideas and paradigms; they play an active role as well. Gottlieb (1987) insists that discourse, rather than being a mere "tool for transferring meaning and intention," actively "shapes what is thought and done" (p. 279). Sarup (1993) states that discourses "are perhaps best understood as practices that systematically form the objects of which they speak" (p. 64). Luke (1995) explains this as the *constructing* character of discourse. There is a "social and ideological 'work' that language does in producing, reproducing or transforming social structures, relations and identities" (Fairclough, 1995, pp. 209–210). B. K. Marshall (1992) defines discourse as "a regulated system of statements that can be analyzed not solely in terms of its internal rules of formation, but also as a set of practices within a social milieu" (p. 99). Woolgar (1988) tells us that the specific discourse of science "is to be understood as [that which] structures and sustains a particular moral order of relationships between the agents of representation, technologies of representation and their respective 'objects'" (p. 14).

Foucault (1972) makes the point that "discourse is not a slender surface of contact, or confrontation, between a reality and a language (langue), the intrication of a lexicon and an experience" (p. 48). Rather, Foucault (1972) takes as his task explicating discourse as "practices that systematically *form* the objects of which they speak" (emphasis added, p. 49). In examining discourse, Foucault is not interested in an explication of the "objective reality" of the subject under study; rather, Foucault is interested in "how texts are constructive of social formations, communities, and individual's social identities" (Luke, 1995, p. 9). As subjects become objectified through discourse, a type of knowledge-power relationship is formulated. Discourse is the power/knowledge nexus. In short, discourses and the discursive practices that give voice to them are social constructions rather than transparent images of reality; as such they have an active and social function. In addition to the constructive character of discourse Ball (1990) explains that "Discourses are about what can be said and thought, but also about who can speak, when, and with what authority. Discourses embody meaning and social relationships, they constitute both subjectivity and power relationships" (p. 2).

When discourse is considered in this critical way, issues of dominance emerge. Teun van Dijk (1993b) defines dominance as "the exercise of social power by elites, institutions or groups, that results in social inequality, including political, cultural, class, ethnic, racial and gender inequality" (pp. 249–250). It is important to note that power is not a unilateral relationship, although in this definition of dominance emphasis is on a "top-down" relation (van Dijk, 1993b). There are also "bottom-up" expressions of power in the form of resistance, complicity, and compliance. However, "our critical approach prefers to focus on the elites and their discursive strategies for the maintenance of inequality" (van Dijk, 1993b, p. 250). The power dimension of educational psychology is discussed further in chapters 4 and 5.

Categories and constructs found generally in discourse, and those found in educational psychology's discourse in particular, are *ascribed* a degree of "truth"; they are understood as a reflection of reality. Disciplines construct and are constructed by discourses that are accepted as "truth" by various communities. Indeed, Foucault (1980a) assures us that "[e]ach society has its regime of truth, its general politics of truth: that is the types of discourse which it accepts and makes function as true" (p. 131). Presently, as has been the case historically, there are multiple discourses within the field of educational psychology (Glover & Ronning, 1987; Scheurman, Heeringa, Rocklin, & Lohman, 1993; Yee, 1970). Each approach expresses a degree of variation. Despite any disagreement, educational psychology is considered a coherent discipline "with its own goals, research agenda, and infrastructure" (Glover & Ronning, 1987 p. 3). There is a dominant discourse of the discipline.

Textbooks

What I do in this book is provide an example of how critical discourse analysis can be applied to the mainstream, dominant discourse of educational psychology. Textbooks are chosen as a valuable area for analysis. The choice of textbooks is based on several issues:

1. Textbooks enjoy a long history of use in the discipline and form a genre of discourse.
2. They are considered an authoritarian source of the discipline's content.
3. Textbooks are used to "pass on" the discipline to future generations of educational psychologists.
4. They present particular problematics.
5. They need to be recognized as social artifacts with multiple constraints.

Each of these reasons for focusing on textbooks will be discussed briefly.

First, beginning with the publication of Edward L. Thorndike's *Educational Psychology* in 1910, educational psychology textbooks are marked by a prolific history, and form the discourse of the discipline. Textbooks are "primary resources for many educational psychology courses" (Anderson et al., 1995). Westbury (1990) states as "truism" the fact that "textbooks are the central tools and the central objects of attention in all modern forms of schooling" (p. 1). De Castell, Luke, and Luke (1989) point to the distinctive status of the textbook as the "primary medium of formal education" (p. viii). Textbooks are accepted as being "an enduring and influential part of schooling . . . they define much of what teachers teach and students learn" (Elliott & Woodward, 1990, p. viii).[7] Squire and Morgan (1990) characterize textbooks as the "bedrock" tool for instruction "since they have demonstrated their convenience and cost effectiveness" (p. 123). In short, textbooks form a particular genre of discourse in and of themselves.

Second, textbooks are perceived to be authoritative sources of a discipline's content. Thomas Kuhn (1970) explains that textbooks "address themselves to an already articulated body of problems, data, and theory . . . [and explicate a particular] set of paradigms" to which a scientific community" (p. 136) is committed at a particular time and place. Educational psychology textbooks have been referred to as "virtual cornucopias of knowledge bases" (Houtz & Lewis, 1994, p. 5) and they "tend to be written from a consensus perspective and, therefore, serve as a valid indicator of what professionals generally regard as important for an undergraduate survey" (Scheurman et al., 1993, p. 100). Olson (1989) explains that written texts "serve an important archival functioning in preserving what the society takes to be 'true' and 'valid' knowledge" and when knowledge is stored in this written form, it "carries great authority because it appears to originate in a transcendental source" (p. 241). A. Graham Down of the Council of Basic Education (quoted in Apple & Christian-Smith, 1991) relates that "[t]extbooks, for better or worse, dominate what students learn. They set the curriculum and often the facts learned, in most subjects" (p. 5).

Third, textbooks are the principal means by which the science is transmitted to future generations and, as such, may be considered "pedagogic vehicles" (Kuhn, 1970). Textbooks fulfill a need to "acquaint the student with what the contemporary scientific community thinks it knows" (p. 140). Apple (1988) asserts that it is the textbook that "often defines what is elite and legitimate culture to pass on" (p. 81). Van Dijk (1993a) suggests that both textbooks and the introductory classes in which they are used be regarded as the initial encounter students have with the discipline. Textbooks advance the "goals, concepts, ideas and theories of their discipline . . . therefore, textbooks not only express the scholarly views of their authors, but obviously shape those of their student-readers" (van Dijk, 1993a, p. 165). Thus, introductory textbooks in education have been characterized as providing a kind of "grammar" (Luke, 1995) for introducing pre-service teachers into the profession of teaching.

Fourth, there is a need to investigate textbooks because they are problematic in several areas. Textbooks are critiqued on the level of genre for becoming increasingly bland and simplistic (Webb, 1995). They have been characterized as slow in responding to changes within the field, in research foci, in presenting challenges to time-honored theories, and so on (Scheurman et al., 1993). However, because of their ubiquity and longevity in the American educational system, they are perceived to be a basic, fundamental, necessary, and neutral element in the teaching-learning process. Indeed, herein lies their power as textbooks enjoy a commonsense acceptance as neutral and necessary. As such, they convey the discourse of the discipline to newcomers to the field, and therefore, play a social role. This social role is significant and complex and presents the most important impetus to examine and interrogate the specific sort of discourse found in textbooks, particularly introductory educational psychology textbooks.

Fifth, the issue of constraints needs to be addressed. While textbooks can be thought of as "collections of statements that make authoritative knowledge *claims*" (emphasis added, Cherryholmes, 1988, p. 52), textbooks need to be appreciated as not just a compilation and articulation of "facts." Textbooks are "conceived, designed, and adhered to by real people with real interests" (Apple & Christian-Smith, 1991, p. 2) who contend with real constraints, and who participate in real relations of power. Even when we appreciate the "evolution" of textbooks as developed and adopted by members of the educational psychology community, it is naive to think of them in their origin, production, or use as neutral. Apple and Christian-Smith (1991) advise that textbooks are "important artifacts" in defining whose culture is taught, whose knowledge is recognized as legitimate and "true." Textbooks signify "particular constructions of reality, particular ways of selecting and organizing that vast universe of possible knowledge" (p. 3). Cherryholmes (1988) has insisted that "Foucault shows textbooks to be political, material products that represent a privileged way of seeing things, privileged by means of power, position, tradition, and so forth" (p. 61). At the heart of Foucault's insight regarding truth as "relational" are the constraints related to the production, sale, and use of textbooks.

Constraints experienced by authors, manufacturers, and consumers are multiple; these constraints are economical, political, ideological, and personal. The witness of Naomi Silverman (1991), who has worked for years as an acquiring editor for a textbook publishing company, can assist our understanding. Silverman states that "textbooks are products that are manufactured and sold for the purpose of making a profit" (p. 163). While other factors play a constraining role, such as interests of the author (Spring, 1991), research advances (Chall & Conard, 1990), course curricula, and new trends, the "bottom line remains constant: Will the book make a profit for the company?" (Silverman, 1991, p. 163).

Silverman further argues that differences of opinion arise between author and editor over issues relating to marketability. This is not a new phenomenon; rather it is a recurring dilemma. She quotes from a 1936 book *Are Teachers Free?* to make her point regarding the continuing tension, "He [sic] wants to tell the truth, and have his authors do the same. Yet he must sell books" (quoted in Silverman, 1991, p. 174). Young (1990) has the same focal point regarding economic constraints of textbooks when she asks, "How can you trust a profit-making industry to do what is best to create textbooks" (p. 72). Joel Spring (1991) recounts his experience of the "political and economic forces shaping textbooks," to which he refers as an aspect of "ideological management" (p. 186). Profit making is not the only concern of textbook publishers, but it certainly is a major driving concern.

The application of a critical analysis to the dominant discourse of educational psychology found in its textbooks springs not only from the fact that textbooks are important "pedagogic vehicles," but also that textbooks supply a succinct compilation of what the discipline considers to be its "heart." More important, critical discourse analysis must be applied because of the political, economic, and ideological nature of textbooks. Without this analysis the societal role of textbooks could remain invisible, and therefore, considered normative, neutral, objective, and "true."

Critical Literacy and Intertextual Reading

Literacy occupies a position of central importance in this mode of critical discourse analysis. Literacy is connected to reading and writing. However, there are several ways to look at these activities. Reading is sometimes understood in the mechanical sense of decoding sounds and words as one develops a skill that facilitates *finding* meaning in the text. The image of *consumption* is frequently connected with reading (Freire & Macedo, 1987). Readers are assigned the position of consumers of the text: readers "chew" and "swallow" (sometimes whole) the words and ideas of the textbooks; they struggle to digest the ideas; readers are encouraged to internalize what they have read, to make it part of them (Woolfolk, 1995). Literacy in this view "very often becomes a matter of mastering technical skills, information or an elite notion of high-status knowledge" (Aronowitz & Giroux, 1991, p. 98). This is what is understood as functional literacy.

Teachers, from this perspective, simply serve as guides to students toward the proper interpretation and implementation of the text, as Scholes (1985) says, "so that the truth might stand revealed" (p. 13). If this is what it means to "read" then the text is given a reverential position as though it were "a vehicle for eternal truth" (Scholes, 1985, p. 13).

This is a limited sense of reading and text, one that fits easily into a transmission model or banking notion of education (Freire, 1992). This type of reading has been implicated in educational psychology textbooks as they are presented as authoritative texts, regarded as containing the paradigms in the center of the discipline. There is a promise extended to students of the discipline that by learning, internalizing, and utilizing the material therein, they can become better teachers. However, Scholes insists that the worst thing teachers can do is to foster an attitude of reverence before texts as if the text were a vehicle for abiding truth.

A critical discourse analysis takes up another sense of literacy. Textbooks are understood as socially connected to and embedded in political, historical, economic, social contexts in which they are located. In other words, any text is involved in a web of other texts. Scholes (1985) expresses this view as *intertextuality*. There must be an examination of these other texts. If intertextuality is ignored or suppressed, then the power of the text as a final authority is magnified. What results is a form of illiteracy.

Sandra Harding (1996) makes a similar point in charging that when scientists and members of the dominant group fail to read even natural science intertextually, as a text within contexts, a scientific illiteracy pervades the social order. Harding (1996) herself presents a countertext exposing, contesting, recasting mainstream scientific discourses.

My perspective is that educational psychologists need to change the way we consider the work of teaching educational psychology. If we desire to dissociate ourselves from a functional and often vulgar literacy, we must change the way we read and teach the discipline. Teachers of educational psychology must analyze and help students analyze the intertextuality of educational psychology. We need to shift our focus in teaching from transmitting the "knowledge" of the textbook to recognizing that the discourses contained in educational psychology textbooks are embedded in other texts, e.g., contexts, pretexts. Necessarily then, the discourse presented by the text becomes a site of social struggle. Our students and we need to engage and criticize educational psychology texts rather than simply consume them.

I am using reading as it has been identified as an active process (Freire, 1985, 1987; Scholes, 1985) of textual power. It is a "productive activity, the making of meaning, in which one is guided by the text one reads . . . but not simply manipulated by it" (Scholes, 1985, p. 8). The position of the reader is understood as the one who makes meaning of the word through a critical reading of the world in which the text is embedded (Freire, 1985).

There is a pedagogy of textual power explained by Scholes (1985) that affects how I read and teach educational psychology. Textual power has three forms of process. Initially, texts have *power over* students (and teachers), a power that is palpable. In the story I recounted in the first chapter, the textbook we were about to study contained the discursive practice around which my student felt such constraint; that which empowered me limited her. There is a stage of submission to the power of the text; this is obvious in my own use of the text as I ascribed to its "truth." I located myself within the text; I shared a semantic and syntactic field with the text; I understood and accepted the particular codes of the text (Scholes, 1985). I was intent on introducing my students to these meanings throughout the course of educational psychology.

The process of *interpretation* follows. This concept entails reading a text along with possible explanations. For example, my student who questioned the practice of pop quizzes subverted the surface power of the text by offering another interpretation. From one perspective it could be argued that she did not know the codes; I tried to explain them to her. Another interpretation on what was happening in the exchange is available; i.e., she was exposing a "division of purpose . . . the return of the repressed" (Scholes, 1985, p. 40). The "student"[8] was responding to the text from her own context, a beginning of intertextuality. The reader's own position forms an important context for reading.

What I was learning was that there are many texts contained in and connected to the particular disciplinary text I was teaching, e.g., political, economic, historical contexts; these produce various interpretations. They become obvious in the codes presented by the text. Indeed, this is the point of my teaching, i.e., "to study the intertextual system of relations that connects one text to others" (Scholes, 1985, p. 31).

The third phase of textual power is *criticism*. Scholes (1985) explains criticism as *text against text;* criticism "provides important opportunities to break with dominant readings and interpretations" (Cherryholmes, 1988, p. 158). Criticism is possible with the differentiation of "the subjectivity of the critic from that of the author, [it is] an assertion of *another* textual power against that of the primary text" (Scholes, 1985, p. 40). Through the act of writing, criticism presents a countertext, a talking back discussed in chapter 2. Scholes notes that criticism "begins with the recognition of textual power and ends in the attempt to exercise it" (p. 41) through writing.

Teaching students how to recognize the codes of a particular text, to analyze them intertextually and present criticism, seems a more appropriate task for teachers than limiting teaching to assisting students in finding the "meaning in" the text. Teachers can help students access the skills "they will need in order to define and shape the modern world, rather than simply serve in it" (Aronowitz & Giroux, 1991, p. 108).

In order to engage the process of critical discourse analysis it is important to read the dominant or mainstream discourse of the discipline. This dominant discourse is found in mainstream texts, those held in high regard and used frequently by those who are involved in teaching the discipline. In the spring of 1995 a survey was sent to a random sample of 210 members of the American Psychological Association, Division 15, Educational Psychology. The purpose of the survey was to have members of the educational psychology community nominate textbooks used in introductory classes that are considered "classic," i.e., those containing the mainstream discourse of the field. The intention in asking this particular group for information was to gather an "emic" perspective, an insider's view (Foster, 1994), of the field.

A return rate of 63% of the surveys was realized. The two textbooks receiving the most nominations were chosen for the critical discourse analysis. They are *Educational Psychology* (1995, 6th ed.) by Anita Woolfolk and *Educational Psychology* (1991, 5th ed.) by Nathan L. Gage and David L. Berliner. These two texts provide the discourse of the discipline, which I examine and critique in the following chapters.

CHAPTER 4

Toward
a Poststructuralist
Analysis

As a student of educational psychology I had "learned" the discipline at one level. It was not until I began "teaching" an introductory course to preservice teachers that I began questioning the discipline. The act of questioning took me to another level of understanding. What I had accepted as "real," "stable," "true," and "neutral" within the discipline's knowledge base I gradually began to read as a "reflection of conventions" (Kincheloe, 1993) imbued with political interests. It was an uneasy reading. As I became aware of the way power and knowledge implicate each other, I began to critique educational psychology's mainstream discourse as a "regime of truth" (Foucault, 1980a).

This chapter begins a critical reading and analysis of the mainstream discourse of the discipline of educational psychology. Through the survey described in chapter 3, two educational psychology textbooks, *Educational Psychology* by Gage and Berliner (1991, 5th edition) and *Educational Psychology* by Woolfolk (1995), were nominated by the educational psychology community as "classic" texts of the field. These texts supplied good samples of the dominant discourse of the discipline.

The analysis presented in this chapter and the next is meant to be an example of a critical poststructuralist analysis. As reflected in discussions in the preceding chapters this analysis is facilitated by an oppositional reading, necessarily partial, and coming from a particular social and political location, i.e., it assumes and acknowledges my own situated knowledge (Collins, 1990; Haraway, 1991; Harding, 1991). It is illustrative and by no means exhaustive. It represents a sample not a synopsis of all possible critiques (Murphy, 1993). It is a counterdiscourse, and serves to "talk back" to and denaturalize the dominant discourse of the discipline of educational psychology.

Two aspects of the discipline of educational psychology are examined in the critical discourse analysis that follows. First, the *disciplinary principles* that form the internal features and particular rationality of educational psychology's discourse are highlighted. Then the *nondiscursive* aspects of the discipline, including the political and social networks in which the discourse is embedded, are examined. These aspects are discussed briefly as the chapter begins.

Disciplinary principles are apparent in the particular rationality, i.e., *technical rationality*, of the discipline. A technical rationality provides the meaning-making system, a kind of internal regulation (Foucault, 1972), of the discipline of educational psychology. It is evident in the rules, relations, and regularities that lie just below the surface of the discourse. This internal regulation is generally considered a resource for the discipline as it provides a "grounding" for the discipline's perspective. It is powerful in that it influences thought and by extension the knowledge and practice of the discipline itself.

While the internal system of the discourse is considered a resource from a particular standpoint, it also can be considered a constraint from another perspective. The technical rationality of the discipline presents *problematics* when read critically. In the use of the word problematics I adopt Foucault's notion of developing something that is accepted (i.e., a given) into a question (Caputo & Yount, 1993). Problematics can remain invisible if the technical rationality of the discipline is "taken for granted" and becomes transparent or invisible, or is considered "natural." Usher (1993) aptly describes the possibility that educational psychologists are "*enfolded* in an implicit conception of disciplines as neutral bodies of knowledge" (emphasis added, p. 17). It is possible that educational psychologists are caught in our own unself-reflexive meaning-making system. Educational psychologists will remain prisoners of the discourse unless we gain access to the constitutive forces of the discipline's rationality.

Educational psychologists, through a critical reading and analysis, can make explicit and interrogate the disciplinary principles of the discipline and the problematics they suggest. Viewed from a critical perspective the science of the discipline in general as well as its truth claims do not cease to exist; instead, "they become representations that need to be problematized rather than accepted as received truths" (Aronowitz & Giroux, 1991, p. 75).

This section of the chapter is an appropriation of Foucault's (1972) notion of archeology, i.e., an investigation of the human sciences as systems of knowledge. Archaeology has been described as a "critical investigation of disciplinary systems of knowledge with the goal of understanding the discursive practices that produce those systems of knowledge" (Prado, 1995, p. 25). Dreyfus and Rabinow (1983) emphasize that Foucault's aim was "to rediscover on what basis knowledge and theory became possible" (p. 17). Once this is understood it is possible to begin to think differently, and to understand "what what we do does" (Foucault, quoted in Dreyfus and Rabinow, 1983, p. 187).

The *nondiscursive aspects* of the discipline are discussed in the second section of this chapter. Nondiscursive aspects pertain to the "background practices" (Dreyfus & Rabinow, 1983), the human activity, and institutional processes operating within the discipline (Foucault, 1972) as well as those within which the discipline is embedded. These include the social, political, economic, and historical contexts and contingencies of the discipline that are prior to the "truth" of the discipline and are potent in the hegemonic[1] construction of the discourse.

Educational psychologists, for example, persevere in the belief that the discourse is developed and controlled through rigorous scientific activity (Cherryholmes, 1988). This activity yields a body of knowledge able to be put to positive use in education. However, this commonsense assumption can "work behind our backs in powerful and constraining ways" (Gitlin, 1990, p. 444). The discipline is embedded in power relationships (Foucault, 1980a). By ignoring these various power relationships, the relationships that enable and facilitate the discipline's discourse and practices (Cherryholmes, 1988), it is possible to take as natural and necessary, as transcendental truth, that which is actually of our own making. As Gergen (1985) insists, "a given understanding that prevails . . . is not fundamentally dependent on the empirical validity of the perspective in question, but on the viscidities of social processes" (p. 268). All the things that are said through the discipline's dominant discourse, what metaphors and values are endorsed, what remains unsaid, and what knowledge is marginalized are actually the result of social negotiations and power relationships more than rigorous scientific activity. As Thomas (1997) points out, what is considered knowledge is "what is *agreed* to be correct rather than the product of compelling justifications" (emphasis added, p. 92).

Disciplinary Principles

What Is a "Discipline"?

A "discipline," in one sense of the word, is considered a "neutral, scientifically validated bod[y] of knowledge whose . . . effects are enlightening and empowering and which thus enable effective action" (Usher & Edwards, 1994, p. 48). David Berliner, a preeminent educational psychologist and coauthor of a "classic" textbook, expresses confidence in the discourse of the discipline as a body of knowledge marked with an empowering character. He asserts: "I think that in the past few years we have come closer than ever before to providing direct scientific underpinnings for the art of teaching. In some cases, the need for highly inventive, creative minds has been lessened, as research provides ideas and technology that are *almost* directly applicable to classroom life" (emphasis in original, Berliner & Rosenshine, 1987, p. 3). He continues: "We now have something that an ordinary person does not have—a knowledge base consisting of facts, concepts, and technology that can transform our profession. . . . Knowledge is clearly power, a kind of social power" (p. 31). Berliner's quotes portray the discipline as producing a body of systematized knowledge that is cumulative; this body of knowledge is produced through the scientific practice of a specific group of persons; and conveys faith that it is able to be applied in positive ways to the practice of teaching. These tenets are implicated throughout the classic texts of the discipline of educational psychology.

Gage and Berliner (1991) have stated in their preface that the purpose of the textbook is "to give prospective and practicing educators . . . an introduction to what educational psychology can provide by way of facts, concepts, principles, and research methods that will be both theoretically enlightening and practically useful. We want our students to take what we present as theory and put it into use in their classrooms" (p. xvii).

Woolfolk (1995) similarly tells readers that "the major goal of this book is to provide you with the best and the most useful theories for teaching—those that have solid evidence behind them. . . . [these theories] are ways of understanding the challenges that teachers face" (pp. 16–17).

Discourses of Disciplines—Sites of Struggle

Textbooks typically present the mainstream discourse of disciplines. A discourse is important in poststructuralist research but for reasons other than those traditionally understood. Poststructuralists are skeptical that knowledge can be systematized because knowledge claims are considered local, partial, and always permeated with power and human interests (Usher & Edwards, 1994). Claims of neutrality are always suspect as discourses, even scientific ones, act in the interests of some persons over others. Therefore, the work of discourse analysis is undertaken not because a discourse is understood as delivering "truth"; rather, a discourse is selected for analysis because its "truth" is seen as relational, situated, and partial (Luke & Gore, 1992), and needs to be understood and critiqued as such.

Discourses are sites of encounter and struggle. McNay (1994) explains: "*Discourses and meaning are the site of social struggle. The process through which hegemonic social relations are achieved and maintained often involves the stabilization of discursive relations and the fixation of meaning. . . . Similarly, resistance to hegemonic meaning entails the contestation and disruption of naturalized forms of discourse*" (emphasis added, p. 75). Once we recognize that the discourse of educational psychology is a site of social struggle we are able to enter the dialogue,[2] to engage in debate, and offer criticism that "provides important opportunities to break with dominant readings and interpretations" (Cherryholmes, 1988, p. 158).

Rationality of a Discipline: Ideology

As stated in chapter 3, a hallmark of modernity is entrusting "reason" as the way to know the "truth," ascertaining universal laws through which order may be maintained. Reason was/is understood as "the source of progress in knowledge and society, as well as the privileged locus of truth and the foundation of systematic knowledge" (Best & Kellner, 1991, p. 2). *Rationality* is the means by which a person or group puts the world in order. In other words, rationality is the sense-making activity of a particular community evidenced in the community's discursive formation. Rationality is evident in the particular views of knowledge, set of interests, beliefs, expectations, meanings, and methodological forms of inquiry that are held by a person or group (Giroux, 1983a). The dominant discourse of educational psychology has a particular rationality, as do other examples of discourse (e.g., feminist standpoint epistemology discussed in chapter 2).

The sense-making function of rationality is akin to a meaning of "ideology." Words like "ideology" are seldom part of the discussions regarding disciplines in the social sciences such as educational psychology. The assumed neutrality of the science eschews words like ideology often considered in a pejorative sense; it is something another group subscribes to, while "we" have, or at least search objectively for, the "truth" (Burbules, 1995). The way ideology forms a perspective, or influences work and relationships, is easily overlooked. As mentioned in the beginning of this chapter, another possible reason educational psychologists rarely consider the ideology of the discipline is that we are so embedded in it that we take the sense-making activity of the discipline as "natural."

The ideology to which I am referring permeates social life—we all participate in it (Giroux, 1983a). Ideology is evidenced in "the production and representation of ideas, values, and beliefs and the manner in which they are expressed and lived out by both individuals and groups" (McLaren, 1989, p. 176). Van Dijk (1993b) explains ideologies as "the fundamental social cognitions that reflect the basic aims, interests and values of groups" (p. 258). This "sense-making" characteristic of ideology is important as it is involved in the "production, consumption, and representation of meaning" (Giroux, 1983b, p. 16). This is the sense of "ideology" I am concerned with here, rather than with specific political ideologies, such as socialism, communism, or conservatism (Giroux, 1983b).

Another characteristic of ideology gives it significance. Ideology's potency only "becomes clear when it is linked to the concepts of struggle" (Giroux, 1983b, p. 16). A critique of ideology, therefore, serves to present the interests of some persons in dialectical relationship to the advantage of others. This is why a critique is "useful and necessary . . . because it helps identify the struggles that are central" (Sarup, 1996, p. 70).

The dynamic of the struggle to be considered along with rationality is expressed through the "problematic" (Giroux, 1981, 1983a). As explained earlier, the problematic represents a questioning of an assumption or belief communicated in the discourse. Problematics have an added dimension in that they also raise questions regarding what is not expressed in the discourse, or what has been silenced by the discourse. In this way problematics reveal "the ideological source that lies beneath the choice of what is considered important and unimportant in a mode of thinking" (Giroux, 1981, p. 9). That is, the way things are understood affects the kind of questions that seem intelligible or important, and, at the same time, puts other questions outside the realm of comprehension or reasonableness. However, questions that seem unfathomable if taken seriously could transform our basic assumptions (Giroux, 1983a); they form a counterdiscourse to the dominant ideology. Therefore, problematics are important considerations.

A particular rationality "grounds" the dominant discourse of educational psychology and is quite evident in the discipline's classic texts. This is explained as a *technical rationality*, which becomes obvious through a close reading of the codes found in the texts of the discourse. Technical rationality is understood as "an epistemology of practice derived from positivist philosophy" (Schon, 1987, p. 3). It has been described as indicative of embeddedness in a "culture of positivism" by Giroux (1981) because it is based "upon the logic of scientific methodology with its interest in explanation, prediction, and technical control" (p. 42). As the natural sciences provide the model for its theoretical development (Giroux, 1983a), it is understandably explained as a "normal-science version of social science" (Schon, 1995); it allows for a kind of "scientific management" (Kincheloe, 1993) of education.

Technical rationality is rooted in the modernist need to control and bring order to an objective world. It operates through the following interrelated assumptions expressed by Giroux (1983a). *Control* is the goal of technical rationality (and therefore, educational psychology's goal), and is made possible through the application of educational theory, or law-like propositions, derived from empirical research. *Discovery of causation* is possible through this scientific management and makes credible the possibility of prediction and control. The knowledge derived from this inquiry is understood as *value-free* and represents neutral, objective reality. Therefore, educators using its knowledge believe they *act in a value-free manner.*

Technical rationality is evidenced not only in the discourse of the texts; it is built into the structures and practices of modern educational activity and educational institutions themselves (Bloland, 1995; Schon, 1995; Usher & Edwards, 1994). In the following discussion, first, evidence is presented to show how technical rationality pervades the discourse of educational psychology (Giroux, 1981) as expressed in its classic texts; second, the problematics provoked by this perspective are discussed.

Control and the Possibility of Causation

The purpose of gaining control of the educational experience is central to educational psychology's discourse found in classic textbooks (e.g., Gage & Berliner, 1991; Woolfolk, 1995). Gage and Berliner (1991) explain that the "objectives of educational psychology, like those of any science, are to explain, predict, and control the phenomena with which it is concerned" (p. 16). Hence, educational psychology is intent on controlling the processes of teaching and learning. Scientific research is the means by which control of educational settings is thought possible.

The primacy and fundamental position of scientific research and theory building is clear throughout both classic texts. Both texts provide a defense against the position that educational psychology is merely an exercise in "common sense." This defense operates to answer the historical critique that educational psychology is "putting what everybody knows in language which nobody can understand" (Welton, 1912, quoted in Grinder, 1970, p. 4). Gage and Berliner (1991) assert that research in educational psychology, like research in the social sciences in general, is of high quality. "Despite popular belief to the contrary, the consistency of results compares favorably with that of the physical sciences. . . . The relationship between variables often are even stronger than those on which some medical practice is based" (p. 28).

In a similar manner, Woolfolk (1995) highlights the research of educational psychology in contrast to common sense. She comments that "frequently the principles set forth by educational psychologists—after spending much thought, research, and money—sound pathetically obvious. People are tempted to say . . . 'Everyone knows that!'" (p. 11). She alerts readers that there is a "danger" in thinking, "educational psychologists spend a lot of time discovering the obvious. . . . When a principle is stated in simple terms it can sound simplistic" (p. 13). Readers are warned that it is not a case of what "sounds sensible" but "what is demonstrated when the principle is put to the test" (Gage, quoted in Woolfolk, 1995, p. 13).

It is interesting to note that despite the attempt to differentiate and privilege "scientific research" over commonsense theorizing, there appears a contradiction in that commonsense is called upon frequently to witness a shared understanding, e.g., "Everyone knows what intelligence is" (Gage & Berliner, 1991, p. 51). "Everyone knows what motivation is, how it makes a difference between resentful boredom at one extreme and ravenous interest at the other" (p. 326). Even as the scientific basis of the discipline is defended, it is imperative that at some point the knowledge claims of educational psychology appear "so correct that to reject them would be unnatural, a violation of common sense" (McLaren, 1989, p. 175). This is when hegemony takes hold, i.e., when that which appeals to common sense is accepted as universal truth (Giroux & Purpel, 1983).

Woolfolk (1995) notes that "research is the primary tool" (p. 16) for understanding teaching and learning. Toward this end "descriptive studies and experimental research can provide valuable information to teachers. Correlations allow you to predict events that are likely to occur in the classroom; experimental studies can help indicate cause-and-effect relationships and should help you to implement useful changes" (p. 20). There is little indication regarding just how little cause-and-effect relationships are possible in the social sciences, although Gage and Berliner (1991) do state that "Good experiments, those that allow for clear causal interpretations, are less likely than we would like" (Gage & Berliner, 1991, p. 25). The confidence in scientific method prevails and is reiterated in an appendix titled "Research in Educational Psychology" that is provided because students "must know how information in the field is created" (Woolfolk, 1995, p. 588).

There are limitations placed on what may be said and not said through the discipline by privileging scientific research over other forms of knowledge. For example, the legitimacy of a complaint by some "parents in low-income areas, whose children often tend to do poorly on intelligence tests" (Gage & Berliner, 1991, p. 72) is recognized. Gage and Berliner (1991) explain that these parents may "believe that teachers and school systems hold hereditarian views [regarding intelligence]. And they [the parents] believe these views lead educators to stop trying to help their children" (p. 72). The perspective that parents offer as the result of their own personal knowledge is discounted by citing a 1967 survey reporting that only "6% of American adults, and only 1 and 2 percent of students and teachers believed that intelligence tests measure only inborn intelligence" (Gage & Berliner, 1991, p. 72). The evidence of this 1967 research study is used to nullify the possibility of merit in an argument coming from personal knowledge of a group.

"Neutral" Knowledge

In a discourse based on technical rationality, knowledge arrived at through scientific means is treated as value-free, representing neutral, objective reality. This is an indispensable tenet of the scientific method. It follows that teachers using the discipline's knowledge are judged as acting in neutral and objective ways.

Gage and Berliner (1991) are clear in stating that *the act of teaching*, in general, is not value-free as "teachers must combine insights from educational psychology with ethical thinking about what is good for their students and for society" (p. 7). However, they also emphasize that ethical discussions are not the concern of their educational psychology text: "But educational psychology, and hence this book, is most concerned with the teaching and learning processes in classrooms. More precisely, we deal primarily with the problems that arise in carrying out the tasks of teaching" (p. 7). They explain that the style of writing found in this textbook, "like most textbooks is . . . neutral and dispassionate" (Gage & Berliner, 1991, p. 7).

Similarly, Woolfolk (1996) reflecting on her purpose in writing textbooks, contends that while other educational psychologists have course goals that include deepening students' "social and ethical understandings . . . [or] capacity to be planful and reflective" (p. 41), she has other goals she considers the "heart" of courses in educational psychology. For Woolfolk the "main goal . . . is to help perspective teachers understand, value, and use the knowledge and processes of educational psychology" (p. 41).

An assurance is expressed that better teaching can result through learning and applying educational psychology. Woolfolk (1995) states: "If you can become a more expert learner by applying the knowledge from this text . . . then you will be a better teacher as well" (p. 10). Woolfolk (1995) explains that expert teachers, "like expert dancers or gymnasts, have mastered a number of moves or routines that they can perform easily, *almost without thinking*" (emphasis added, p. 5). Consider the quote from Berliner and Rosenshine (1987) at the beginning of this section, "In some cases, the need for highly inventive, creative minds has been lessened" (p. 3).

Problematics

The discussion of technical rationality in this section has the purpose of displaying the sense-making activity of the discourse. Because discourses are recognized as sites of social struggle, they need to be interrogated. This interrogation is necessary not just to argue or to interpret on the level of ideas, but because theoretical choices have implications for practice (Luke & Gore, 1992). Problematics are posed regarding the following issues: the relationship of theory and practice; a reductionist focus of the discipline; the teachers' role; the limitation of questions and behaviorism; and the possibility of neutral, value-free knowledge.

Relationship of Theory and Practice

There is an implicit understanding that the theory generated in the name of educational research can be applied directly to the practice of education. This is especially clear in each of the classic textbooks as disciplinary knowledge is placed in a foundational position to the practice of teaching. "We have presented a view of educational psychology as a foundation discipline that helps to accomplish the tasks of teaching" (Gage & Berliner, 1991, p. 47); "My goal in writing this book . . . [is] so you will have the foundation for becoming an expert" (Woolfolk, 1995, p. 18). Thus, both the vital role that disciplinary knowledge plays (Giroux, 1981), and the one-way relationship of theory-to-practice (Carr & Kemmis, 1986) are highlighted in these classic textbooks.

Many of the criticisms of the foundational understanding of the relationship of theory and practice regard the decontextualized learning of theories and concepts and then applying them directly to practice (Anderson et al., 1995). The theoretical knowledge is sometimes judged to be inaccessible, or too "scientific" for practitioners. However, the foundational model has proved to be resistant to arguments leveled against it. Despite criticisms, it has been difficult to disconnect from the "formative power" psychology has had on education (Usher & Edwards, 1994). What is it that the foundational model provides that keeps it viable in the midst of so much criticism?

The foundational metaphor is meant to convey a sense of security in that "grounding our thinking about practice on a simplified and scientifically accurate foundation should make it more comprehensible and reliable" (Doyle & Carter, 1996, p. 24). The need for security is heightened as the practice of teaching is recognized as a serious and complex enterprise. This is the optimistic message expressed in both classic textbooks and the dominant discourse of the discipline in general.

Thinking about the knowledge of the discipline as foundational also serves to establish a certain hierarchical order within the discipline. A foundational approach distances those who do research from those who teach it and from those who learn it and eventually apply it to practice. By privileging theoretical knowledge over the practical knowledge of teachers, students, and parents, the conventional power arrangements within the educational process are supported. Also supported are the inequalities constructed by its knowledge claims in a way "so powerful it is almost invisible" (Cherryholmes, 1988, p. 98). These issues will be taken up in chapter 5.

Reductionist Focus

Technical rationality's aim of gaining control through the development and application of theory is advanced when variables can be manipulated in the interest of bringing about "a certain state of affairs or to prevent its occurrence" (Giroux, 1981, p. 43). In order to complete experimental activities, through which theories and principles can be formulated, variables need to be reduced to simplest terms. Necessarily, this directs attention toward the "trivial—on that which can be easily measured by empirical instruments" (Kincheloe, 1993, p. 129). The "illusion" of certainty in practice is supported, but as Kincheloe (1993) remarks, "[r]arely do the most significant questions of human affairs lend themselves to empirical quantification and the pseudocertainty that often accompanies numbers" (p. 129). The underside of reductionism is that it may "simplify a particular phenomenon so as to mask its complexity" (Leistyna et al., 1996, p. 36).

A plain example of reductionist thinking is found in the material regarding writing objectives that are categorized as cognitive, affective, or psychomotor. Both texts recognize the impossibility of separating these areas from each other: "none of these kinds of activities is isolated from the others. . . . The three types of objectives are intertwined" (Gage & Berliner, 1991, pp. 42–43); "In real life, of course, behaviors from these three domains occur simultaneously" (Woolfolk, 1995, p. 447). However, they are separated in these texts, because "it often is useful to focus on one at a time" (Gage & Berliner, 1991, p. 43). In what way is this useful? For whom is this useful? This distinction, "devised by a group of educational measurement experts" (Gage & Berliner, 1991, p. 43), is a "fiction that we tell to make our lives as educators simpler" (Apple, 1994, p. x). These distinct categories have made their way into the realm of a commonsense understanding of educational psychology. They are examples of simplistic ways of understanding phenomena that masks their complexity.

An important issue in this criticism is the emphasis on the efficiency of action, or the "means," by which the control is produced, not on the value of the goal of the practice itself. This implies a separation of factual information intended to facilitate teaching from questions of values that is indicative of technical rationality's goal of gaining control through mastery of theory. The concern is with how to do things, and how to do them more efficiently, rather than on what it is that should be done. Teachers internalize this logic of efficiency.

Teachers as Functional Problem Solvers

Teachers-as-problem-solvers is a favorite role of teachers expressed in classic texts: "Whatever your situation, the tasks you must accomplish raise problems that teachers have always had to face. And these problems arise in some form from the first day and every day you teach. . . . Educational psychology serves teachers . . . by helping them deal with these problems" (Gage & Berliner, 1991, p. 7). Woolfolk (1995) highlights this bias regarding the teacher as a problem solver by playing off Schon's (1983) call for a more "reflective practitioner." Because Woolfolk is discussing the "artistry" of teaching and the need for teachers to be reflective, inventive, and creative she suggests that her readers might find this discussion "a bit idealistic and abstract" (p. 9). She then submits that "[r]ight now, you may have other, more down to earth, concerns about becoming a teacher. You are not alone!" (p. 9). For Woolfolk the more pertinent concerns of beginning teachers include: "maintaining classroom discipline, motivating students, accommodating differences among students, evaluating students' work, dealing with parents" (p. 10). These are the issues of educational psychology. Students of the discipline are told that "by applying the knowledge from this text . . . you will be a better teacher" (p. 10). Anything that keeps teachers from their task of efficiently solving technical problems is apparently considered secondary.

Two important themes can be inferred from Woolfolk's (1995) discussion. First, the "real" concerns of teachers are defined and delimited by those who write the texts. These become the issues in which educational psychology can be useful to teachers; these are the problems and solutions addressed in the text that are to be learned and internalized by readers. Second, focus is directed away from the need of teachers to be reflective about the work that they do and the ends for which teachers teach. The focus becomes the problem-solving activity.

Kincheloe (1993) refers to the "how-to" emphasis as an example of "crude practicality" that characterizes so many technically

oriented teacher education programs. Cherryholmes (1988), likewise, alerts us to a "vulgar pragmatism" that is "instrumentally
and functionally reproducing accepted meanings and conventional organizations, institutions, and ways of doing things for
good or ill" (p. 151). Teachers in this perspective are seen primarily as instrumental problem solvers who "select technical means
best suited to a particular purpose" (Schon, 1987, p. 3). This
image of teachers constructs a specific view by which a "technical ethos is created which eventuates in. . . . a constricted view of
teacher cognition, which reduces the act of teaching to merely a
technique" (Kincheloe, 1993, p. 10).

It is ironic that through an enculturation into the discipline,
through internalizing the mindset of educational psychology,
teachers can become complicitous in their own de-skilling
(Apple, 1993; Giroux, 1983a; Kincheloe, 1993; Macedo, 1994).
Even so, teachers are not necessarily so "malleable and powerless
that they submit to their own victimization" (Giroux & Purpel,
1983). People do have and can be encouraged to be reflective, to
develop a sense of the social, political, and historical contexts in
considering the mainstream discourse of this discipline. Teachers
can be self-reflexive and realize that there are multiple texts that
support and facilitate, or contest and interrogate, particular
meaning-making systems. However, the discipline itself supports
and privileges thinking within the established paradigm.

Limiting of Questions

Technical rationality limits the kind of questions that may be considered legitimate within the discipline. Questions are confined to
those that have a specifically technical solution, those that can be
addressed through scientific research. Questions about "problems" that teachers face have to be handled within an empiricist
tradition and, therefore, need to be reduced to variables that are
treated in isolation. This manner of thinking "creates a form of
tunnel vision in which only a small segment of social reality is
open to examination" (Giroux, 1981, p. 46). Ignoring complexities
is in sync with Edward L. Thorndike's (1910) recommendation in
an early educational psychology textbook. He stated in a discussion of laws of learning that "The complexities of human learning
will in the end be best understood if at first we avoid them" (p. 6).

Besides limiting questions to those that can have technical

solutions, questions are also transformed or recast as problems with technical solutions. Thus, issues regarding the social, cultural, and political situations that arise in educational institutions and classroom life are explained through "neutral" scientific means. This allows for a very subtle entrenchment of hegemony as scientific justification provides for the ideal solution to social, political, and ideological problems (Apple, 1990).

Problems dealing with diversity in tracking, for example, are managed as scientific issues. Through the use of scientific technologies of testing of "intelligence" the differential control of access to high status knowledge is not seen as a power play of agents of the dominant culture, but rather rationalized as the commonsense dealing with the varying "abilities" of students.

Behaviorism, for another example, is effective in advancing the empiricist perspective of technical rationality in that it is concerned with efficiently controlling the environment through the manipulation of discrete (and often minute) variables. A commitment to a behavioral perspective is presented as a commitment to efficiency and effectiveness, but it can also express a commitment to control, manipulation, and a vulgar pragmatism (Cherryholmes, 1988).

Classic texts manifest their behavioral proclivities in the perspective they present in several areas. Although theories other than behavioral ones are covered to some extent, the preponderance of space and endorsement is afforded to the behavioral perspective. A small sampling communicates this bias.

Gage and Berliner (1991) provide a good illustration in their definition of "learning," as "a process whereby an organism changes behavior as a result of experience" (p. 225). They go on to state that "it is the overt behaviors of talking, writing, moving and the like that allow us to study the cognitive behaviors that interest us—thinking, feeling, wanting, remembering. . . . The overt behaviors of the organism—pigeon or school-age child, dog or teacher are always our starting point" (p. 225). Social interactions between teacher and students are described as "two or more people stimulating and responding to one another" (p. 503). The handling of a category of behavior described simply as "too much," "calls for extinction or punishment" (p. 511); behavior of the "too little" variety "calls for reinforcement, which strengthens behavior" (p. 512).

Personality is described as "a concept derived from behavior. We see only behavior. But we create names for that behavior to talk about the different kinds of behavior we notice" (p. 147). Gage and Berliner (1991) go on to explain that "we need to emphasize more that behavior is controlled, to a large degree, by the way rewards and punishments occur in the environment" (p. 148). In the discussion of "motivation" the authors explain that their text explores "the operant-conditioning approach to the understanding and improvement. This approach concentrates on the environment—particularly the reinforcement contingencies in the environment" (Gage & Berliner, 1991, p. 327).

Despite a reliance on behaviorist psychology, Skinner is mentioned only in citations in Gage and Berliner (1991). The knowledge claims and practices of this perspective appear ahistorical or transhistorical with no mention of the social or political context that influenced its popularity in the 1940s and 1950s in the United States. The role of teacher as "social engineer," which characterizes Skinner's theoretical perspective (Sprinthall & Sprinthall, 1990), might be unpalatable to teachers yet that is the implication of the behavioral approach. Although teachers should be able to evaluate and question theories, this is difficult to do because of the assumption of neutrality and objectivity, the authoritative tenor of the text, the limiting of questions, and the emphasis on technical problem solving.

Texts as Neutral and Value-Free

Giroux (1981) comments that generally, values are dismissed as inappropriate for discussion from a perspective embedded in technical rationality. Questions of value must be eschewed within a technocratic worldview as values are thought to weaken the scientific process. Giroux (1981) explains: "Information or 'data' taken from the subjective world of intuition, insight, philosophy and nonscientific theoretical frameworks is not acknowledged as being relevant. Values, then, appear as the nemeses of 'facts,' and are viewed at best, as interesting, and at worst, as irrational and subjective emotional responses" (p. 44). Although classic texts claim a stance of value-free neutrality, they can be read as expressing very clear values, usually the values of the dominant culture. These values are presented as normative and natural. Value statements appear so frequently that their authors subvert their own claim to neutrality.

Values are revealed in what is included and what is excluded from texts, and the type of rhetoric connected with issues. For example, Gage and Berliner (1991) expound on the effectiveness of small class size and cite studies supporting this assertion. They proceed to add another value factor, cost-effectiveness, to the discussion. They conclude: "Knowing that smaller classes are more effective and creating them are two different things. A major problem is cost" (p. 502). They report that it would cost $34.5 million to reduce class size by one, from 30 to 29. Readers are presented with the conclusion that "reducing class size at all grade levels from 30 to 15, to obtain substantial improvement in education, would increase the cost even more" (p. 502). The unreported message is that this cost is more than "we" would want to pay. This position displays a stark contrast to the critique of the "savage inequalities" in funding educational resources exposed by Kozol (1991). It also assigns cost-effectiveness as a premier value in education, over quality and equity. This value-laden assertion ignores the political and economic issues related to the fact that some school districts can and some cannot "afford" small class size. In accepting as a matter of course that small class size is just not "feasible" inequality becomes "naturalized."

Another example of values being very much an aspect of purportedly neutral texts is obvious in the discourse expressing the differential treatment of students. It is the discourse of scientifically solving problems, so characteristic of technical rationality, that allows discussions like the following to be viewed as acceptable within "neutral" discourses.

Woolfolk (1995), for example, presents a discussion of between-class ability grouping as a way to make teaching *more appropriate* for students" (emphasis added, p. 118). However, the text states that there are several "problems" with the practice of ability grouping. The following problems are listed:

Lower ability classes seem to receive lower-quality instruction in general. Teachers tend to focus on lower-level objectives and routine procedures. There are more management problems. Teacher enthusiasm and enjoyment are less in the lower-ability classes. . . . [and]

lower expectations are communicated to students. Student self-esteem suffers almost as soon as the assignment to "dummy" English or math is made. Attendance may drop along with self-esteem. The lower-tracks often have a disproportionate number of minority-group and economically disadvantaged students, so ability grouping, in effect, becomes resegregation in school. (pp. 118–119)

The problems connected with ability grouping are attributed to "difference in instruction and/or the teachers' negative attitudes" (p. 119). These problems are attributed to technical difficulties with tracking. Even with the listing of problems of such a profound nature, the practice of ability grouping itself is represented as neutral and remains unproblematic. The real violence done to students seems invisible or trivialized as this method of instruction is conceptualized as "more appropriate."

The importance of this issue is further minimized by the little attention that is given to examine the consequences of this grouping on students' daily lived experience of schooling. A single paragraph is used to report these negative effects. The complexities of the social struggles that produced the current configuration of practices and how these practices fit relations of ruling in the wider society (Rizvi, 1993) remain obscured.

Only if the instructor chooses to present the information in the background section (located in the margins, printed in light blue, and available only in the teacher's edition), is the educational psychology class offered a brief summary of a well-known and important research program. *Keeping Track: How Schools Structure Inequality*, originally published in 1985 by Jeannie Oakes,[3] discusses the deleterious effects of ability grouping and tracking, and, more important, places the issue within its historical and social context. However, this material is not readily available to students who are using this text.

Gage and Berliner (1991) address the issue of ability grouping in a section titled "*Coping* with Individual Differences" (emphasis added, p. 449). The situation of individual differences among students is reported to have "complicated" the teacher's task (Gage & Berliner, 1991). The discourse presents certain individual differences as a "problem" to students of educational psychology, something that will need coping with and an issue that will complicate their life as a teacher.

Again, a technical solution to the "problem" of individual differences is presented, and it is based on the assumption of innate ability: "to set each student to work on tasks appropriate to his or her particular abilities and interests. . . . appropriate to the student's temperament. . . . to move each individual ahead at his or her own rate" (pp. 449–450).

Ability grouping is presented as a step toward individualized instruction. The idea behind this method of instruction is that "teaching is *more effective* with students of similar ability" (emphasis added, p. 450); even so, it is noted that conflicting results have been reported regarding "achievement, self-concept, attitudes toward others, and behavior" (p. 450) in employing this teaching strategy.

Gage and Berliner (1991) also refer to the findings of the Oakes (1985) research (mentioned above). The text states, in reference to this study, that "ability grouping has been suspected, and often found guilty, of fostering social-class discrimination: Lower-income students wind up in one group; higher-income students in another" (p. 450). The assignment to low-track is even characterized as a "life sentence" (Gage & Berliner, 1991). Once again, the practice of ability grouping of students itself remains unproblematic; it is characterized as a "plausible" way of coping "with individual differences in *stable* characteristics . . . (scholastic abilities, interests)" (emphasis original, p. 450).[4] How is it that the discourse can reconcile the admission of such negative effects as *more effective* and *plausible*?

Contrastingly, another group of students, i.e., gifted and talented, receives quite a different presentation: "Gifted and talented students contribute greatly to society and should be considered a precious human resource. Our investment in identifying and developing these students should at least rival—in interest, time, and money—the investment we make in gifted athletes" (Gage & Berliner, 1991, p. 217).

Woolfolk (1995), like Gage and Berliner (1991), asserts the importance of providing for the special educational needs of "gifted" children.[5] The characterization of gifted students by a former secretary of education as "our most neglected students" is repeated. Gifted programs formulate yet another "track" allocated for students who "contribute greatly to society and should be considered a precious human resource" (Gage & Berliner, 1991, p. 217). These "remarkable individuals" (Woolfolk, 1995) are represented as a scarce commodity that must be developed for our national security and well-being (Sapon-Shevin, 1993).

Through the discourse of educational psychology such differential valuing and treatment of children is authorized and perpetuated despite conflicting effects and long-standing accusations that ability grouping does not work (Slavin, 1987), is not fair (Oakes, 1985), and is undemocratic (Giroux & McLaren, 1989). Nevertheless, ability grouping continues to appear reasonable and is accepted as tolerable from within the meaning-making system of the discipline. General acceptance of this practice as a commonsense way to organize schooling experiences is achieved through the work of the discourse.

The discourse constructs the situation in such a way that the semblance of neutrality and meritocracy is upheld.[6] This understanding is promoted by assigning children to ability groups on the basis of the assumption of the biological reality of innate ability, i.e., "intelligence."[7] Since innate ability can be determined through the use of "neutral" standardized tests, the social stratification that results from this differential access to curriculums appears efficient, reasonable, and is taken as common sense. The historical, social, and political contexts in which students' access to curriculums is sorted and selected is cast as scientific and value-free.

An uncritical reading of the dominant discourse contained in classic texts does not engage the complexity of meaning or examine the value-laden aspects of issues that are seen, at first glance, as "neutral" and acceptable. In contrast to the traditional understanding of the discipline's discourse as a neutral body of information, a critical reading presents the discourse of educational psychology as a site of struggle. Meanings in the discourse can be contested and struggled over, and they are. Even so, the dominant discourse prevails. To more fully understand why the discourse exists as it does, it is necessary to look beyond disciplinary principles to the "effects of power [that] shape a discursive practice" (Cherryholms, 1988, p. 59). The effects of power are infused in the nondiscursive background practices that precede the text and talk of educational psychology. They are the human, social, institutional activities that make the discipline possible in the first place (Dreyfus & Rabinow, 1983). These nondiscursive practices are presented in the remainder of the chapter.

Nondiscursive Practices of Educational Psychology

In chapter 1, I used Foucault's (1980a) idea of discourse of a modern science, such as educational psychology, as a "regime of truth." Foucault's famous quote deserves repeating: "Truth is a thing of this world: it is produced only by virtue of multiple forms of constraint. And it induces regular effects of power. Each society has its regime of truth, its 'general politics' of truth: that is, the types of discourse it accepts and makes function as true" (Foucault, 1980a, p. 131).

Understanding the discipline of educational psychology as a "regime of truth" contrasts with the view of the discourse of the discipline as a neutral body of scientifically validated knowledge. In discussing the discourse as a "regime of truth" it is important to foreground and interrogate those social, political, economic, and institutional networks in which the discipline is embedded. Discussions need to be taken up concerning the relationship of power and knowledge; the social construction of knowledge; the impossibility of neutrality of knowledge; the division of labor in knowledge production highlighting a power hierarchy regarding as to who controls knowledge production and whose meanings are legitimated.

Power–Knowledge

Understanding that "knowledge is power" within a traditional perspective of educational psychology contrasts with what Foucault means in the quote above. The traditional contention is that the development of the knowledge of the discipline (i.e., the discipline's "truth") has given educational psychologists power. The relationship is understood as *causal:* knowledge causes power. The "direct scientific underpinnings . . . the knowledge base consisting of facts, concepts, and technology" (Berliner, 1987, p. xvii) give educational psychologists power. In other words, use of the technical knowledge of the discipline gives one knowledge. For Foucault (1995) the relationship of power and knowledge is correlational: "power and knowledge directly imply one another: . . . there is no power relation without the correlative constitution of a field of knowledge, nor any knowledge that does not presuppose and constitute at the same time power relations" (p. 27). Foucault, therefore, always refers to power and knowledge together, i.e., power-knowledge,[8] a "solidus [suggesting] that for his purposes power and knowledge are not to be studied separately" (Sarup, 1996, p. 72). They are "immanent in one another, each a condition for the possibility of the other" (Usher & Edwards 1994, p. 87).

Power relations pervade the knowledge-making activity, affecting the one who knows, that which is known, and the mode and practice of knowing (Foucault, 1995). The implication of this relationship of power–knowledge for the human sciences is that the "truth" expressed by the discipline is both produced and confined by the power relationships of the discipline. In other words, "truth" is what the discipline says is "truth." As Usher and Edwards (1994) point out, knowledge "does not simply represent the truth of what is, but, rather, *constitutes* what is taken to be true. . . . It's what counts as true that is important" (emphasis added, p. 87).

Aronowitz (1988) pushes this power–knowledge dynamic a step farther. He insists that "The power of science consists, in the first place, in its conflation of knowledge and truth" (p. vii). The truth that is being produced by the specific scientific manipulations of the discipline is a specialized knowledge that has been conflated with truth.

When the understanding of how power and knowledge implicate each other is recognized, a radically different perception of knowledge follows. What counts as knowledge is considered the "truth" of the discipline. However, this truth is also understood as the product of social activity imbued with power relations. There is always a political struggle over knowledge, and it is not something that resides solely in the realm of ideas. Rather, it is a matter of mechanisms of power that are prior to discourse and often unspoken. These mechanisms decide who may speak, when, and what may be said; this is a "general politics of truth" (Foucault, 1980a, p. 131) that pervades the discipline. Thus, the knowledge of any discipline can never be received as neutral; it is always situated, contingent, and partial and the result of social struggle.

The Social Construction of Knowledge

The way the world is known and explained is the result of "historically situated interchanges among people" (Gergen, 1985,

p. 267). This pertains to scientific knowledge. Scarr (1985) insists that we "should not be disturbed that science is constructed knowledge. Rather, the recognition of our own role in scientific knowledge should make more modest our claim to truth" (p. 500). Nevertheless, those who do science have consistently failed to examine the social practice of producing knowledge and the historical, economic, and political context that give it meaning in the first place. It seems as though at times educational psychologists have forgotten that they have "invented the knowledge they apply. . . . they do not discover, they invent" (Caputo & Yount, 1993, p. 7).

The mainstream educational psychology community may not recognize that the dominant discourse contained in classic texts has been socially constructed. A textual style of narrative realism and the appearance of consensus lend to the discourse the ambience of objective knowledge.

Textbooks are usually written through a textual strategy of *narrative realism* (Usher & Edwards, 1994) that accentuates the "reporting of already existing ready-made reality" (p. 150). Using this genre the text is understood as a "neutral medium for conveying pre-existing facts about the world. . . . [its] neutrality exempts it from consideration as a species of social/cultural activity" (Woolgar, quoted in Usher & Edwards, 1994, p. 150). This strategy also allows the text to appear as an authoritarian source of what the discursive community considers the truth of the discipline (Kuhn, 1970). Rizvi (1993) describes this as a type of "rhetorical appeal that is by its very nature uncritical" (p. 137).

Narrative realism is effected frequently by statements made in a matter-of-fact style. Gage and Berliner (1991), for example, state: "It became possible during the twentieth century to measure individual differences in intelligence" (p. 50). This simple statement masks the historical and political context and struggle in which the statement is embedded.[9]

An argument could be made that there is some evidence in the mainstream discourse that the knowledge of the discipline is recognized as the result of negotiated understandings within the educational psychology community. This is because the pronoun "we" is used throughout both textbooks. For example, Gage and Berliner (1991) explain that:

> A concept is the organized information *we have* (emphasis added) about an entity. . . . The meaning, boundaries, and relationships connected with a concept are derived from everything *we know* (emphasis added) about that concept. . . . What *we mean* (emphasis added) by a concept is partly a matter of definition and partly a matter of the methods of studying the concept. . . . for example, the meaning of the concept of intelligence depends in part how *we define* (emphasis added) *intelligence* (emphasis in the original). (pp. 12–13)

The "we" of this discussion could be referring to the educational psychology community, Gage and Berliner being "author-ized" (Usher & Edwards, 1994) to speak in its name. However, it is more likely that it is the editorial "we" that is reflected here and throughout the text. This makes it difficult to know to whom the text is referring. Contrary to Gage and Berliner's assertion, there is no universal agreement among educational psychologists about a construct as complex and politically charged as "intelligence" let alone with other educationalists or the general public.[10] However, their use of the pronoun "we" builds the impression that there is universal agreement. Apple (1993) remarks "the very use of the pronoun 'we' simplifies matters all too much" (p. 49).

The continual use of the editorial "we" serves to create the illusion of consensus around an "objective" discourse of educational psychology. There is an attempt to build what Rizvi (1993) calls a "collective phenomenon." Van Dijk (1993b) points out that consensus building is a major function of any dominant discourse. In a climate of consensus, acceptance and legitimacy of knowledge allow a particular discourse to dominate and achieve hegemonic control.

Textbooks and the discourse they support need to be understood as important artifacts of culture (Gergen, 1985) that "signify through their content and form, *particular* constructions of reality, *particular* ways of selecting and organizing the vast universe of *possible* knowledge" (emphasis added, Apple, 1993, p. 49). At any time there are competing discourses, competing paradigms, and their respective proponents can be imagined as "practic[ing] their trades in different worlds. . . . [they] see different things when they look at the same point in the same direction" (Kuhn, 1970, p. 150).

Gage and Berliner (1991), for example, recognize that deliberations related to the construct of intelligence are connected with "different social and political ideologies" (p. 51). They are clear in presenting the definition that they support, characterized as "traditional," i.e., "Intelligence = what tests measure" (p. 51). Readers are told that this definition stems from "the intellectual tradition of the developed nations" (p. 53). Gage and Berliner (1991) explain that this tradition is "only one approach to human learning and instruction—namely, that appropriate to a middle-class segment of an industrialized society in which learning takes place in a certain kind of classroom in an institution called school. If *our* society were different . . . we would probably have to redefine intelligence" (emphasis added, p. 53). Even while both texts acknowledge that there is no agreement on what intelligence really is (Gage & Berliner, 1991; Woolfolk, 1995), their perspective on intelligence is utilized as the standard perspective.[11] This traditional psychometric perspective is privileged as it is presented as neutral, normative, and unproblematic. There seems to be no recognition of the psychometric perspective's alignment with any social and political ideology through which students are included, excluded, or marginalized in schools and in society on the basis of such measurements.

In summary, although there is a growing acceptance of knowledge as a social construction (e.g., Gergen 1985; Kincheloe, 1993; Scarr, 1985), it is questionable whether traditionally educational psychologists have recognized the knowledge claims of the discipline as socially constructed. The genre of narrative realism generates the appearance of consensus and neutrality in textbooks. These can be considered a "pre-text" (Usher & Edwards, 1994) that needs to be interrogated and subverted as there is a "hidden politics of neutrality" (Kincheloe, 1993, p. 42). It is the impossibility of neutrality of knowledge that is discussed next.

The Impossibility of the Neutrality of Knowledge

The claim of neutrality of knowledge needs to be discussed. As mentioned earlier, neutrality can be used as a "cloak" covering scientific research. As long as knowledge is considered neutral, it can claim a place separate from human interests, biases, and power.

The fact that knowledge can never be neutral is an assertion that crosses disciplinary lines and epistemological stances. Those who offer a feminist critique of science (e.g., Bleier, 1984;

Harding, 1991; Hubbard, 1989; Namenwirth, 1986) join critical educational theorists (e.g., Apple, 1993; Freire, 1992; Giroux, 1981, 1983a; Kincheloe, 1993; McLaren, 1989), and feminist poststructuralists (Luke & Gore, 1992) in this assertion. McLaren (1989), for example, challenges traditional ideas regarding the neutrality of knowledge: "Knowledge acquired in school—or anywhere, for that matter—is never neutral or objective but is ordered and structured in particular ways; its emphasis and exclusions partake of a silent logic. Knowledge is a *social construction* deeply rooted in a nexus of power relations" (emphasis in the original, p. 169). Even so, the claim of "neutrality" is a strong and important condition for the human sciences. It is the representation of the knowledge of a discipline as neutral and objective that facilitates an assumption of certainty and universality. In this way the knowledge of educational psychology is able to function as a foundation on which to base practice or as a resource that informs practice. However, as Giroux (1981) explains, this view of knowledge "not only undermines reflective thinking, it does this and more. It is also a form of legitimation that obscures the relationship between "valued" knowledge and the constellation of economic, political, and social interests that such knowledge supports" (p. 53). When the acceptance of the neutrality of knowledge is subverted, a whole new discernment is required. If knowledge cannot be accepted as neutral, a demand follows to know more about the political implications that permeate it. New questions surface concerning whose interests does the knowledge serve? Whose experience is legitimated or marginalized? Who profits through this knowledge?

Many critical educational theorists have written persuasively on this subject. Banks (1993) has explained that "knowledge that people create is heavily influenced by their interpretations of their experiences and their positions within particular social, economic, and political systems and structures of a society" (p. 5). Apple (1993) asserts that "what counts as legitimate knowledge is the result of complex power struggles among class, race, gender, religious groups" (p. 46). It is not a question of what knowledge is of most worth, rather it is *whose* knowledge (Apple, 1993, 1996) is privileged and made to appear "natural," "normal."

Alison Dewar addresses the question of "whose" knowledge is normative. She explains succinctly: "The knowledge we teach in our educational system has a white, middle class, androcentric bias. More importantly, this bias is not presented as one possible version of reality, but more often is taught as the only, legitimate and therefore, representative version of reality" (Dewar, quoted in Lewis, 1992, p. 42). This white, middle-class, androcentric knowledge is the knowledge that counts (Sleeter & Grant, 1994), and this is the knowledge that "provides formal justification for and legitimation of prevailing institutional arrangements" (Anyon, 1978, p. 40, quoted in Giroux, 1981, p. 53). Generally this is the knowledge found in textbooks (Banks, 1993; van Dijk, 1993a).

It is often easy to discern the bias of whose knowledge gets privileged in the dominant discourse of educational psychology. Numerous examples attest to this fact in educational psychology's mainstream discourse. One example is obvious, again using the psychometric understanding of intelligence. Gage and Berliner (1991) admit that "A society will always have a problem testing the intelligence of minority-group members because, by definition, they do not belong in important ways to the majority culture that usually develops the tests" (p. 54). In the very next sentence these authors state simply: "We measure intelligence with tests" (Gage & Berliner, 1991, p. 55). Later in the chapter Gage and Berliner (1991) state that, "Because minority-group and poor children less often do well on these tests, their parents have a right to worry about how the information from the tests is used" (p. 74). Indeed, assignment to a "slow group early on can be like a *life sentence with no likelihood of parole*" (emphasis added, p. 74). Children who belong to economically disadvantaged groups and especially when they are also part of a minority are essentialized and seem almost alien (Rizvi, 1993). This kind of representation also presents the dominant group as homogenized. There is a clear admission that this normative practice of psychometric testing in the discipline benefits those in the dominant culture.

This situation is naturalized by being represented as "the way things are." Note Gage and Berliner's (1991) assertion: "A society will always have a problem testing certain groups of children." The assumption is that it could not be otherwise (Rizvi, 1993). Thus, this purportedly "neutral" discourse functions to sustain the power relations of the status quo. More important, it trivializes the violence done to children through testing procedures. Mainstream educational psychology has left the concrete reality of oppression in many children's lives unchallenged.[12]

The Division of Labor in Knowledge Production

Implied in the above discussion is the existence of a hierarchy of power (van Dijk, 1993b) in the production of the knowledge of the discipline. There are some who speak with authority; they are "author-ized" to speak. Others must listen. van Dijk (1993b) refers to the former group as the "power elites," i.c., those who have "special access to discourse; they are literally the ones who have the most to say" (p. 255). The elites of the discourse have a particular social power.

Social power could be understood as involving control of one group over others regarding acts in limiting freedom, or cognition, i.e., how people think (van Dijk, 1993a, 1993b). The social power referred to here is primarily concerned with the cognitive aspects of power that involve knowledge production, or "managing the minds of others . . . a function of text and talk" (van Dijk, 1993b, p. 254). Although the idea of "managing minds" may be startling, it is the latent purpose of the dominant discourse of educational psychology. The dominant discourse is aimed at initiating novices into a particular meaning system, i.e., "facts, concepts, principles, and research methods that will be both theoretically enlightening and practically useful" (Gage & Berliner, 1991, p. xvii).

Those who are considered authorities purport to clarify meaning. Meanings that are accepted generally are understood as *social cognitions* (van Dijk, 1993b). These social cognitions influence "beliefs, understandings, attitudes, ideologies, norms and values" (van Dijk, 1993b, p. 257). Clearly, classic textbooks take this as a goal, i.e., reproducing social cognitions by supplying meanings and definitions for various concepts.

Teachers of educational psychology may accept their task as "transmitting" the meaning of the discourse to students. Students are, in a sense, positioned as receivers of knowledge, "consumers" of the dominant discourse presented in textbooks. Of course, the teaching-learning process is more complex than simply determined by the reproductive metaphor. On the one hand, students of educational psychology are active participants in their own learning, and their learning could never be determined by these texts. My student in the opening story is a good example. On the other hand, the rationality of the dominant discourse does steer students in the direction of particular interpretations.

As the discussion on narrative realism pointed out, meanings in textbooks often appear to be fixed; they are presented as objective and static. "Textual" features are used to reinforce these meanings. The Gage and Berliner (1991) text supplies a glossary that provides "brief definitions of key terms" (p. xx) and marginal notes "highlighting important points . . . quick guides to key ideas and issues" (p. xix). Woolfolk (1995) furnishes readers with a margin glossary that "defines terms of the text to provide *easy access* to the terms and their relevant examples as the student studies" (emphasis added, p. ix).

A poststructuralist analysis problematizes the idea of meanings as fixed. What is necessary is recognizing how power infiltrates language (Cherryholmes, 1988) constructing social cognitions. Cherryholmes insists that: "Culturally sanctioned, positive, and authoritative knowledge is incomplete, interest-bound, tied up with existing power arrangements, and cloaked in certainty. As the illusion of certainty is dispelled, it becomes possible to uncover the origins and commitments of our structures and the effects of power that led to their production" (p. 70). Modern textbooks bear the effects of power and represent a privileged view of the material they present. The school knowledge they contain "reveals which groups have power . . . [and] which groups are not empowered by the economic and social patterns in the society" (Anyon, 1983, p. 49). These become obvious in omissions, stereotypes, and distortions that are found even in updated versions of textbooks (Anyon, 1983). Consider the following examples of stereotypes regarding Native American cultures: "Some place high value on the skills required in weaving. Some of them depend on spearfishing for much of their food. If industrial society valued these skills in the same way, our educational system would focus on them and our definition of intelligence would give them greater importance" (Gage & Berliner, 1991, pp. 53–54). There are several problematic assumptions in this statement; one is that all members of given groups share the same cultural and behavioral patterns (Sleeter & Grant, 1994). This refers not only to the minority groups, but the assumption pertains to the dominant groups as well. Do all Native Americans groups weave and fish? What about the economic, social, and cultural contexts in which members of groups weave and fish—or do not? How do the authors use the word "our" to exclude persons considered outside the group in power? Another implication is that the minority group is deficient in comparison to the dominant culture, i.e., industrial society, that determines the type of tests given in the society. These assumptions, though erroneous, serve to reinforce stereotypes, perpetuate social cognitions, and disguise oppression or power relations.

Meanings attributed to "race" are especially noxious and significant. Gage and Berliner (1991) note that "race" "typically should refer solely to such psychologically unimportant characteristics as skin color, eye shape, and facial configurations" (p. 79). Woolfolk (1995) defines "race" as: "A group of people who share common biological traits that are seen as self-defining by the people of the group" (Woolfolk, 1995, p. 165).

The essentializing of race as a stable and biological characteristic persists in both texts, although this representation is generally considered anachronistic within the scientific community (Harding, 1996). It continues to be used in some discourse communities despite the fact that all scientific attempts to show any biological definition of race have been exposed as untenable. This representation persists. The biological representation is useful, however, as it serves to perpetuate the prevalent social cognition of race as fixed. This has a *naturalizing effect* that constitutes social, cultural, and political differences among people *as if* these differences were merely the effect of nature.

There is a professed "disinterest" in "race" evident in the Gage and Berliner text through its representation of race as referring to characteristics that are "psychologically unimportant." Again, this representation is useful as it limits how readers think of race by taking it out of social and cultural contexts. In this way the understanding of meritocracy that is based on individual merit, hard work, and achievement (Haymes, 1996) can be preserved.

How is it that stereotypes and incorrect information continue to be presented in current textbooks? The possibility of the effects of power relations must be considered. Some individuals may dominate a field, not because of their arguments but because of their positional authority (Cherryholmes, 1988). What is important to recognize is that often those considered the "elites" of the discourse may "enact, sustain, legitimate, condone, or ignore social inequality or injustice" (van Dijk, 1993b, p. 252) supported by the official knowledge of the discipline. Thus, knowledge in a dominant discourse needs to be interrogated as the "property of an elite establishment working to maintain its power" (Usher & Edwards, 1994, p. 198). When this is understood, it facilitates a critical position in both teachers and students.

The work of this chapter focused on beginning an interrogation of the dominant discourse of the discipline of educational psychology using two classic textbooks. The first part of the chapter discussed disciplinary principles understood in terms of technical rationality. These principles, although supplying a grounding of the discipline, are rarely examined. Although often considered a resource, they also constrain the discourse of the discipline and, therefore, are problematic and need to be interrogated. The remaining portion of the chapter considered the non-discursive aspects of the discipline that include the social and political contingencies in which the discipline is embedded.

This discussion is important not solely on the level of ideas. The meaning-making system and power relations of the discipline are important because they affect the everyday discursive practices of schooling and the material conditions of children's lives. These practices are the focus of chapter 5.

CHAPTER 5

Disciplining the Discipline

This chapter[1] takes as its focus an examination of the practices sanctioned by educational psychology's dominant discourse and investigates the effects of these practices. The discussion of Chapter 4 regarding technical rationality and the nondiscursive power–knowledge relationships of the discipline facilitates the turn to this focus. This turn is imperative as the ideas generated by the meaning-making structure evident in the discursive principles of educational psychology "gain strength and are a form of power [because] . . . they take concrete shape in the actions of our daily lives" (Freire & Faundez, 1992, p. 26).

Through the process of education students are "socialized" so as to adapt to the world. Students are judged, labeled, sorted, and selected according to how well they fit in. Through its knowledge base and practices the discipline of educational psychology claims to explain characteristics of the student and the teacher; the assertion of the discipline is "to know those objects truthfully . . . [by their] 'natural characteristics'" (Usher, 1993, p. 18).

Using the perspective of Foucault, a different view of socialization is proposed. Foucault is skeptical regarding modern disciplines, especially those connected with education (Ball, 1990). Foucault's position is that knowledge of the modern disciplines is organized around the power to define and name others—especially to define persons as *normal* and as *abnormal*. Human beings are defined and made subjects of the society through the process of *normalization* often understood as *socialization*.

The knowledge and the practices of the human sciences are central to this process. Through their specific knowledge claims and practices, human beings are thought to be simply described and categorized. The language used to convey the reality of the person is considered neutral and unproblematic in itself. However, from a critical perspective language is considered to have a productive characteristic; it is through the language, the discourse, of the discipline that subjects are formed and constituted.

Modern sciences through their specialized knowledges produce a new subject, a subject[2] of a particular kind (J. D. Marshall, 1990), i.e., subjects who are docile and useful. Foucault's contention is that every modern discipline is "a general formula of domination" (1995, p. 137). Thus, the knowledge of modern discipline "ceases to be a liberation and becomes a mode of surveillance, regulation, discipline" (Sarup, 1993, p. 67). The specific disciplinary practices derived from the knowledge claims of educational psychology are implicated and interrelated in the processes whereby societies control and discipline their populations (Philp, 1985) through the educational process.

Foucault's idea of the meaning of the human sciences as "disciplines" is a central theme in this chapter. The contemporary understanding is tied to the former meaning of discipline, i.e., it is concerned with the control of bodies. The understanding of "trope" discussed below helps illuminate this connection. A discussion of the formation of the discipline follows beginning with an appropriation of Foucault's concept of *genealogy*. Foucault uses genealogy to explicate how every historical era has sought control over populations, changing only the strategies through which control is achieved. The human sciences are the current means through which control is gained. Next, three disciplinary technologies are presented that Foucault suggests form the basis of the disciplinary practice, i.e., *hierarchical observation, normalizing judgment*, and *examination*. These disciplinary practices are utilized by disciplines to normalize students and are located in the everyday activities of school life. Finally, I use these disciplinary technologies to inform my critical reading of the dominant discourse of educational psychology expressed in two classic textbooks.

A thorough examination of these various points is important in order to render visible what has been taken for granted, i.e., to make the familiar strange (Foucault, 1995). The presentation of the everyday practices can and must be looked at differently because "as soon as one can no longer think things as one formerly thought them, transformation becomes both very urgent, very difficult, and quite possible" (Foucault, 1988, quoted in Dales, 1992, p. 83).

Discipline: Control of Bodies

One meaning of "discipline" is discussed in chapter 4. "Disciplines" are discussed as they are usually considered "neutral, scientifically validated bodies of knowledge whose only effects are enlightening and empowering and which thus enable effective action" (Usher & Edwards, 1994, p. 48). However, this chapter takes up a different meaning of discipline. The word discipline can be understood more fully through a consideration of "trope." Tropes are words in which new meanings contain residues of former uses of the word; new meanings are understandable in connection to the original sense of the word (Briscoe, 1993). Tropes help us notice what could have been missed without their recognition; they make our thinking swerve (Haraway, 1996) and we are able to "see" things differently.

In thinking about discipline as a trope it is helpful to consider its various lexical meanings:

1. Training expected to produce a specific pattern of behavior. . . .
2. Controlled behavior resulting from disciplinary training.
3. A systematic method to obtain obedience.
4. A state of order based on submission to rules and authority.
5. Punishment intended to train or correct.
6. A set of methods or rules [that regulate] practice. . . .
7. A branch of knowledge or of teaching. (Soukhanov, 1984, p. 383)

It is not until the sixth and seventh meanings that a match is found for our commonsense understanding of the word "discipline" used in the context of a "body of knowledge." Educational psychology, for example, as a discipline and branch of psychology includes laws, principles, theory, and practice aimed at improving teaching and learning. However, recognizing discipline as trope helps one appreciate Foucault's meaning of "disciplinary power"; it is important to see the connection with the other meanings listed for the word "discipline."[3] The discipline, the human science, of educational psychology is connected with managing and controlling the bodies of students, e.g., behavior. The recognition of the dynamic relationship among power, knowledge of the discipline, and the control of bodies is necessary for understanding the practices of educational psychology.

In *Discipline and Punish* Foucault (1995) connects the control of the body and the growth of the scientific knowledge of disciplines since the seventeenth century. Foucault studies the spread of "disciplinary mechanisms . . . [as] techniques through which modern societies train and regulate individuals" (Sarup, 1996, p. 72). In modernity, as "objective" science developed so did "a radically new regime of power/knowledge" (Fraser, 1989, p. 22) through the discipline's discourse. This shift in regimes of power from the classical age through modern times will be discussed later in the chapter. However, it is important to emphasize here that the aim of the disciplinary technologies remains the same, i.e., the control of the bodies of human persons.

Foucault explains two manifestations of power over the body. One manifestation is *bio-power*, a "modern form of power . . . characterized by increasing organization of population and welfare for the sake of increased force and productivity" (Dreyfus & Rabinow, 1983, pp. 7–8). Dreyfus and Rabinow explain that bio-power is so ubiquitous that it appears as a "strategy, with no one directing it and everyone increasingly enmeshed in it, whose only end is the increase of power and order itself" (p. xxvi). This modern form of power is a control and regulation of the masses, a kind of macropolitics. However, it did not emerge as a coherent management process. It was preceded by Foucault's other manifestation of power, micropolitics.

Micropolitics developed as administrators in various institutions were faced with the daily government of large numbers of people. The historical process of growing and shifting populations, for example, was connected to the formation of the disciplines (Smart, 1985). In order to manage and control the growing number of those in their charge "a variety of 'microtechniques' were perfected by obscure doctors, wardens, and schoolmasters in obscure hospitals, prisons, and schools. . . . only later were these techniques and practices taken up and integrated" (Fraser, 1989, p. 22). In other words, specific tactics were "invented and organized from the starting points of local conditions and particular needs . . . in piecemeal fashion" (Foucault, 1980b, p. 159). Only later were these procedures gathered to form a coherent discourse.

An example of the development of the local conditions generating specific practices can be found in writings about the history
of educational psychology. Hilgard (1996), for example, notes
that in the later part of the nineteenth century before educational theory and teacher education became "centered in the uni-
versities, most of the adaptations of education . . . were made by
. . . school administrators" (p. 992). Hilgard's recounting of the
work of William Torrey Harris (1835–1909) is instructive here.
Harris was superintendent of the St. Louis, Missouri, school dis-
trict as the Civil War was ending, a time of increased industrialization and immigration to the area. Hilgard (1996) explains the
need for specific procedures to manage the burgeoning numbers
of children in the schools of St. Louis:

> The problems of school buildings, school management, and teacher
> training loomed large as the heterogeneous population expanded, and
> Harris took seriously his efforts to provide universal education on an
> efficient and effective basis. He did this by adopting the graded school
> so that the curriculum could be planned according to the movement
> of pupils through school, with careful records of attendance, of ages at
> leaving school, and of the progress of learning. (Hilgard, 1996, p. 992)

The specific procedures, or micropolitics, utilized by Harris (i.e.,
graded classes, records of attendance, and progress of students)
imposed an order or governmentalitism on the schooling of children in a particular time and locale. It was much later that these
practices, and others were gathered and generalized into an integrated system of management.

Another notable example of the development of a tactic of micropolitics is the development of the first so-called "intelli
gence" tests by Alfred Binet (1857–1911) and his student Theo-
dore Simon (1873–1961). Universal education, mandated in
France in the nineteenth century, meant that all French children
be given several years of public education (Fancher, 1985). It is
noted that for the first time "retarded children [were included],
who in earlier years would have dropped out early or never attended school at all" (Fancher, 1985, p. 69). A diagnostic tool was
thought to be needed to identify children who "could not profit
from instruction in the regular public schools in Paris" (Lewontin, Rose, & Kamin, 1996).

In 1904, Binet and Simon responded to this local need and formulated an intelligence test and scale. Binet's original intention

was to "construct an instrument for classifying unsuccessful school performers" (Mensh & Mensh, 1991, p. 23) into different groups: idiots, imbeciles, and "debiles" or "weak ones," later translated to "moron" in America (Fancher, 1985).[4] Sorting students in this way, bringing a kind of "order" to the educational system of the time, was a function of the tests.

Later, the scales of Binet and Simon were appropriated for a variety of uses in the United States. For example, the army used variations of the test during World War I "not primarily for the exclusion of intellectual defectives . . . but rather for the classification of men in order that they may be properly placed in the military service" (Yerkes, quoted in Fancher, 1985, pp. 117–118). Postwar analyses of the results helped frame the rationale of the Immigration Act of 1924 defining immigrant groups thought suitable to become U. S. citizens. The testing movement is also linked to the passage of a series of sterilization laws declared constitutional by the Supreme Court in 1927 (Lewontin et al., 1996).

Not long after these applications, educational institutions adopted the tests as a tool for studying individual differences in order to make "formal schooling a *successful and rewarding experience for the whole school-age population*" (emphasis added, Jensen, 1987, p. 61). According to students' "ranking" in tests they could be sorted into "appropriated instructional programs . . . [that] can make it possible for the vast majority of children to attain at least the basic scholastic skills during their years in school" (Jensen, 1987, p. 86).

The point that needs to be clear is that the discourse of the discipline of educational psychology did not emerge self-contained and coherent. The shift in demographics led to the need to govern growing student populations on local levels, micropolitics. Gradually, the formalization of the practices of management was established. Of particular importance were the practices of sorting students. This was deemed necessary to bring order to local school situations. The demographic shift was precipitated by the shift toward industrialization and growth of capitalism and formed a particular historical conjuncture with an emphasis on increased production and efficiency.

There is another historical process occurring at the same time, referred to as a juridico-political process (Smart, 1985). The juridico-political historical process refers to the formal and legal structures of societies that were established around the existing

power relations of the eighteenth and nineteenth centuries simultaneous to the demographic shifts that were occurring. This
process of modern lawmaking took over the power of the sovereign of premodern times. The juridico-political process that developed guarded the status of the group wielding political power.
An example of this historical process can be found in the contradiction of the framers of the U.S. Constitution. At the same time
that freedom was guaranteed to all, provisions recognizing and
protecting slavery were also included (Bell, 1997).

This is the milieu in which the growth of scientific knowledge
gains importance. The scientific historical process refers to the
increasing complex relationship between the formation of
knowledge and the exercise of power.

The Formation of Disciplinary Practices

Foucault is skeptical about the ability of modern human sciences
to fulfill the dream of linear progress. He bases his skepticism on
the "historical evidence . . . that what looks like a change for the
better may have undesirable consequences" (Sawicki, 1991,
p. 27). Foucault offers the *genealogy* as a way to critique totalizing discourses of modern sciences. The genealogist "is a diagnos-
tician who concentrates on the relations of power, knowledge,
and the body in modern society" (Dreyfus & Rabinow, 1983,
p. 105). The genealogy that Foucault presents is a particular history, clearly not history in the usual sense. Foucault (1980a) asks
us to see a genealogy as a "kind of attempt to emancipate historical knowledge from that subjection, to render them, that is, ca-
pable of opposition and of struggle against the coercion of a theoretical, unitary, formal and scientific discourse" (p. 85).

Sawicki (1991) explains genealogy as resistance that "involves
the use of history to give voice to the marginal and submerged
voices that lie 'a little beneath history'—the voices of the mad,
the delinquent, the abnormal, the disempowered" (p. 28). The
purpose of highlighting these subjugated and disqualified knowledges is both "modest and profound . . . to disrupt commonly
held conceptions about events and social practices rather than to
proffer, from on high, proposals for reform" (p. 62).[5]

Foucault (1995) in *Discipline and Punish* presents the genealogy of the prison. Foucault believes that the prison is the "most

characteristic of disciplinary institutions, one which schools, factories, and hospitals all come to resemble" (Shumway, 1989, p. 133). It is Foucault's intention that his history of "the birth of the prison" can or "must serve as a historical background to various studies of the power of normalization and the formation of knowledge in modern society" (p. 308). Normalization and a particular knowledge of each student are key aspects around which educational psychology is organized.

Foucault (1995) explains that every society had its means of control of the body. He describes this control within the historical recounting of the birth of the prisons beginning with the classical age, through the reform era, and arriving at the formation of the modern penal system.

In the *classical age* Foucault (1995) recounts the torture of Robert Francois Damiens, accused of trying to assassinate Louis XV, in 1757. The story delineates torture as a means whereby the sovereign is able to reinstate his authority, with public torture being a kind of political ritual (Dreyfus & Rabinow, 1983). The brutality of the torture is fierce. The punishment leaves its marks, literally, on the body of the condemned who is the subject of the sovereign. The retelling of this torment, however, is meant as an exercise in defamiliarization (Shumway, 1989); the cruel torture is obviously of another era. One finds oneself thinking, "We've come a long way from such barbarism!"

Foucault continues with a review of the eighteenth-century reforms for the punishment of crimes and criminals. This is the *era of reform* in which public torture decreases. The body of the wrongdoer continues to be visible to the public. However, the accent in this era is the restoration of the social contract, with penalties meted out according to the crime committed (i.e., the punishment for murder was death; arrogance was punished by humiliation; the lazy person was sentenced to hard labor). The "corrections" notion was put in place as each "punishment would function as a deterrent, a recompense to society, and a lesson, all immediately intelligible to criminal and society" (Foucault, 1995, p. 148). The body in this era is marked, but marked differently than in the classical age. The body bears the representation of the evil of the crime (Shumway, 1989). Hester Prynne's wearing of the "scarlet letter" in Hawthorne's novel is an apt example.

Describing the crime accurately was of utmost importance in this era of reform. Only in knowing the crime exactly could the proper punishment be given, and the correct ordering/reordering of social life made possible. Precise knowledge of the crime and the criminal allowed for "reformers . . . to construct a comprehensive table of knowledge in which each crime and its appropriate punishment would find its exact place" (Dreyfus & Rabinow, 1983, p. 149).

Foucault reports that the model for this kind of individualization was taking place in natural history of the late eighteenth century. He refers to the prison reforms as a "Linnaeus[6] of crimes and punishments, so that each particular offense and each punishable individual might come, without slightest risk of any arbitrary action, within the provision of a general law" (Foucault, 1995, p. 99). Knowing the crime and the criminal exactly emphasized the importance of the practice of representation. The marks on the body of the classical model are replaced by "signs, coded sets of representation" (Foucault, 1995, p. 130) in the reform period.

The third era of development within the penal system is the *modern model*. Foucault (1995) refers to it as "the gentle way" where "power must act while concealing itself beneath the gentle force of nature" (p. 106). This development is characterized by the appearance of the physical building, the prison, where economy and morality were combined (Dreyfus & Rabinow, 1983) in the methodical use of time (e.g., timetables were enforced and strict horaria were kept) and space (e.g., isolation in cells).

Prisoners were isolated from the rest of society as they were to be feared by society and more easily controlled behind the prison walls. Solitary confinement within the prison was added, so as to facilitate penitence by the prisoners for their transgressions. All activities of the prisoner's day, including required work for economic reasons, were under strict surveillance. The acquiring of exact knowledge of the prisoner was very important and made possible through "dividing practices": separating prisoners from society and often from each other; separating the person of the prisoner into segments, e.g., the crime, intention, or psychological state of the prisoner. In this way, reform was sought to affect the "soul" of the prisoner in the resocializing effort.

Distinct breaks appear with the reforms of the previous era in this third model of punishment. The focus is on the modification of the prisoner's behavior, rather than public representation of a violation and punishment. The primary aim becomes the reform of the soul of the transgressor. The body in this era is like a machine (Shumway, 1989), and the success of the incarceration depended on the training and production of a "docile" and useful body (Dreyfus & Rabinow, 1983). However, it was really the soul that was being formed and reformed. Instead of the common-sense understanding of the soul as the prisoner of the body, what Foucault wants to emphasize is that the body is actually the prisoner of the soul. The control of bodies remains the primary goal of state control. The means of this control is the "gentle way" as the soul internalizes the rules and codes of the society. It is through the conversion of the soul that the body is reformed and conforms, and thereby is rendered docile and useful.

In summary, Foucault (1995) explains in *Discipline and Punish* how, in modern times, the focus has shifted from the overt control of the body, exemplified by monarchial power (Sarup, 1993) to another distinct form of control, although it is still focused on the control of the body. This shift is characterized by an exercise of power over the body that is covert; it is constant, regular, efficient, and unseen. Foucault (1995) characterizes it as the "gentle way" of control, yet it is every bit as potent as the control of former eras.

Disciplinary Technologies

Foucault's major concern is the way modern modes of power form and reform individuals. It is a process of normalization often disguised as socialization. The socializing process is a key effort and effect of institutions and is facilitated by the disciplines of the human sciences.

Foucault (1980c) understands disciplines as "systems of power" with particular "structures and hierarchies . . . inspections, exercises and methods of training and conditioning" (p. 158) that have been "developed, refined, and used to shape individuals" (J. D. Marshall, 1990, p. 15). Disciplines of educational institutions, not unlike the prisons described by Foucault, exercise a kind of bio-power, a modern form of power. This is accomplished in the "increasing ordering of all realms under the guise of improving the welfare of the individual and the population. . . . a strategy, with no one directing it and everyone increasingly enmeshed in it" (Dreyfus & Rabinow, 1983, p. xxvi).

Foucault's *gentle way* is an apt description of this control through a discipline's normalization of students, as they are rendered docile and useful. The dominant discourse of educational psychology, although using other words, seems to concur with normalization as the goal of the discipline as it is stated: "Because education is aimed at *causing* wanted changes in people—in their knowledge, skills, and attitudes—the discovery of ways to cause these changes has great practical importance" (emphasis in the original, Gage & Berliner, 1991, p. 14). This perspective of causing "wanted" changes echoes what Thorndike (1910) asserted as the discipline was developing in the beginning of the twentieth century: "The aim of education is. . . . changing [the student] for the better—to produce in him the information, habits, powers, interests and ideas which are desirable" (p. 4).

The "way" to cause these "changes" is the stuff of educational psychology, its knowledge claims and practices. The normalizing practices of the discipline are utilized to render bodies docile as the individual is "subjected to habits, rules, orders, an authority that is exercised continually around him and upon him, and which he must allow to function automatically in him" (Foucault, 1995, pp. 128–129). Freire (1992) critiques this goal of modern educational practice: "the educated man is the adapted man, because he is better 'fit' for the world. . . . the purposes of the oppressors, whose tranquility rests on how well men fit the world the oppressors have created, and how little they question it" (p. 63). Foucault (1995) specifies disciplinary practices as the technologies of *hierarchical observation, normalizing judgment,* and the *examination.* These major disciplinary "technologies" are understood as the "methods which made possible the meticulous control of the operations of the body that assured the constant subjection of its forces and imposed upon them a relation of docility-utility" (Foucault, 1995, p. 137). Even so, they are very simple instruments. Perhaps it is their simplicity that makes them so effective.

Each of the three disciplinary technologies will be presented next. A discussion of the way these disciplinary technologies pervade the discipline of educational psychology follows.

Hierarchical Observation

Hierarchical observation is the disciplinary technology understood as a kind of "optics of power" (Dreyfus & Rabinow, 1983).

It signifies the alliance between visibility and power (Smart, 1985). It is both a literal and a figurative observation. The purpose of requiring that individuals be visible is to make it possible to know them; when people are known they can be changed, thus controlled and rendered docile. First in importance is determining the "nature" of the person, or seeing the individual as he or she really is.

Foucault (1995) explains the importance of understanding the significance of architecture to this optics of power. The palace, for example, was built in the classical era to be seen, a symbol of the sovereign ruler; the fortress was built in such a way as to allow those inside to observe the space external to it. However, the school (as well as the prison) was constructed "to render visible those who are inside it . . . to act on those it shelters . . . to make it possible to know them, to alter them" (p. 172). The schoolhouse, then, became figuratively and literally an apparatus of observation, a kind of "microscope of conduct" (Foucault, 1995). Through observation, knowing, and training the socialization (read normalization) of students can take place.

The ideal situation is a single eye of authority seeing everything constantly (Smart, 1985). As numbers grew in school situations it became increasingly difficult for a "single eye" to supervise all students. A division of the work of the optics of power, or a system of "super-vision," developed as a "disciplinary gaze" that took the form of a hierarchy of continuous and functional surveillance (Smart, 1985). The example discussed earlier of William Torrey Harris initiating the graded schoolhouse is a useful reference for this system of supervision. As students in the one-room schoolhouse could no longer be supervised effectively by one person because of growing numbers, they were separated into the grades, and the graded school appeared. Several teachers watched over their separate grades, and a supervisor watched over them. Foucault (1995) refers to hierarchical observation as the continual play of "calculated gazes."

Surveillance is an important aspect of hierarchical observation. Foucault (1995) introduces the image of the *panopticon* to demonstrate the efficiency and potency of surveillance used in prisons. The panopticon of Jeremy Bentham (1748–1832), the English philosopher and reformer, was meant to produce the effect of "the state of consciousness (and permanent visibility) that assures the automatic functioning of power" (p. 201). Bentham's model called for a central watchtower surrounded by tiered rows of cells. Light from windows in each cell and an open space facing the center tower allowed for prisoners to be in the constant view of the supervisor.

The economy of this mechanism is a major feature of the panopticon's usefulness. The panopticon allowed for the constant surveillance of each prisoner and, at the same time, did not require constant surveillance of each prisoner. Because prisoners knew that they *could* be watched at any time, they never could be sure *when* they *were* being watched. The economy and effectiveness of this model was exacerbated as the prisoners began to internalize the gaze of the supervisor; they watched themselves.

Foucault (1995) tells us that this mechanism, a form of hierarchical observation sets up a "network of relations from top to bottom, but also to a certain extent from bottom to top and laterally; this network 'holds' the whole together and traverses it in its entirety with effects of power that derive from one another: supervisors, perpetually supervised" (pp. 176–177). The internalization of the gaze of the supervisor is extremely significant in the formation of the subject. This internalization has implications for teachers as well as students. Teachers know that they are under the watchful eye of administrators as well as subjected to public scrutiny. Teachers, too, internalize the gaze of those in authority and of the dominant culture; they learn to watch themselves. To be effective and economical, the cooperation of those who are watched must be enlisted.

Normalizing Judgment

Hierarchical observation allows for judgment and evaluation, and the basis of judgment is the *norm*. The technology of normalizing judgment is said to be at the heart of any system of disciplinary power (Foucault, 1995; Smart, 1985). Disciplinary practices need standards around which their operations can be organized so individuals and groups are assessed by "comparisons with a favored paradigm real or imagined" (Prado, 1995, p. 61).

Normalizing judgment has the simultaneous action that marks its power; that is, it assumes and imposes homogeneity and simultaneously introduces individuality:

> The power of normalization imposes homogeneity, but it individualizes by making it possible to measure gaps, to determine levels, fix specialties and to render differences useful by fitting them into one another. It is easy to understand how the power of the norm functions within a system of formal equality, since within a homogeneity that is the rule, the norm introduces, as a useful imperative and as a result of measurement, all the shading of individual differences. (Foucault, 1995, p. 184)

Persons are recognized as individuals when they are described in terms of the norm and with reference to the norm finer and finer differentiation and individualization are possible. Through the normalizing judgment, behavior can be quantified and ranked as it falls on a field between two poles, normal and abnormal, good and bad (e.g., grades on tests, student cooperation, effective and ineffective teachers). A continuum is established and subjects can be placed along it in an objective manner. Foucault (1995) tells us that it has become possible through the modern sciences to "quantify this field and work out an arithmetic economy based on it" (p. 180). More specifically, "an objective hierarchy can be established by which the distribution of individuals is justified, legitimated and made more efficient" (Dreyfus & Rabinow, 1983, p. 158).

A system of penalties and rewards is effective in establishing and supporting normalization. Punishments are exacted for the slightest deviation from the norm, referred to as micropenalties. Micropenalties grew to include more and more areas of life (Dreyfus & Rabinow, 1983). Examples of micropenalties include issues around the following: time (e.g., lateness, absence), activity (e.g., inattention, lack of zeal), behavior (e.g., impoliteness, disobedience), speech (e.g., idle chatter, insolence), body (incorrect gestures, attitudes, cleanliness), sexuality (e.g., impurity, indecency) (Foucault, 1995).

The "Examination"

The "examination" is at the "heart of the procedures of discipline" (Foucault, 1995, p. 184). It combines the other two disciplinary instruments, hierarchical observation and normalizing judgment, into what Foucault (1995) calls the "normalizing gaze." This is the disciplinary technique in which can be found "a whole domain of knowledge, a whole type of power" (p. 185) that allows for differentiation, classification, and judgment of its subjects. Foucault (1995) considers this technology as a kind of tiny, slender, widespread "ceremony of objectification" (p. 187). As such the examination marks a definite exemplification of the connection between power and knowledge.

Increased visibility is a key effect of the examination. Foucault reminds us that in feudal times the most visible people were the most important people, e.g., the king, the epic hero. With the rise of modern sciences the common folk are the ones who become visible as they are subjected to the mechanisms of objectification through the examination. This disciplinary technique of examination has the power to bring the individual into view, able to be seen in multiple ways and with finer and finer differentiation from others.

An important issue in this is that the examination is the "gaze" of the one with more power upon the one with less or no power (Shumway, 1989). The visibility of the subject, or student, is heightened as more and more features of the person are tested and a gathered into a file.[7] Individuals become "cases" through the gathering of common occurring attributes and differences (Smart, 1985), a case that can be described and analyzed, known, categorized, and eventually reformed.

The way Haraway (1991) highlights the metaphor of vision is helpful here. She insists that the visualizing technologies, exemplified in the examination, "are without apparent limit; the eye of any ordinary primate like us can be endlessly enhanced. . . . Vision in this technological feast becomes unregulated gluttony" (pp. 188–189). Haraway insists that vision is always embodied. The eyes that see belong to/in somebody. This understanding exposes the impossibility of a "gaze from nowhere." The image of the eyes of the knower as always embodied renders problematic the claim of modern scientific methods that profess to "factor-out" or "control-for" the personality and bias of the scientist as the results or findings are understood to speak for themselves. On the contrary, the only possibility is vision from somewhere, from somebody, i.e., situated knowledge discussed in chapter 2.

The effectiveness of the disciplinary technique of the examination is intensified through an inversion of visibility; as the individual becomes more visible the disciplinary power itself becomes invisible. Foucault (1995) explains:

> Disciplinary power . . . is exercised through its invisibility; at the same time it imposes on those whom it subjects a principle of compulsory visibility. In discipline it is the subjects that have to be seen. Their visibility assures the hold of the power that is exercised over them. It is the fact of being constantly seen, that maintains the disciplined individual in his subjection. And the examination is the technique by which power, instead of emitting signs of its potency, instead of imposing its mark on its subjects, holds them in a mechanism of objectification. (p. 187)

Thus, despite its potency, the technology of power that facilitates the rendering of subjects as objects is itself invisible, i.e., the productive character of the examination is itself invisible, even as it renders its subject visible. In its ubiquity the normalizing activity of the examination is not questioned. The necessity of the examination in its multiple forms is a commonsense practice; it is taken for granted, considered natural or normal, as though things could not be otherwise.

Through the technology of the examination classifications and comparisons of persons become possible along increasingly finer gradations. Individual differences become significant. Foucault highlights the point that the modern individual is a historical achievement. Subjects are the products of the disciplinary power by which subjects are objectified, analyzed, and fixed (Dreyfus & Rabinow, 1983). Modern sciences have yielded the individual who is both the effect of power and the effect of knowledge, an example of questionable progress, from a "dubious science" (Foucault, 1995). This is a key example of what Foucault calls the productive aspect of power: "We must cease once and for all to describe the effects of power in negative terms: it 'excludes,' it 'represses,' it 'censors,' it 'abstracts,' it 'masks,' it 'conceals.' In fact, power produces; it produces reality; it produces domains of objects and rituals of truth. The individual and the knowledge gained of him belong to this production" (p. 194). In other words, professionals in the discipline produce the knowledge they apply, "they create the knowledge they require in order to fashion functioning, well-formed individuals" (Caputo & Yount, 1993, p. 7). Through this normalizing technology students become objectified; they become their "scores" as they receive their "marks."

This is an inversion of a modernist understanding that knowledge of the subject emerges through the technologies of the discipline. Subjects are *inscribed* by the technologies of the discipline rather than *described* by them.

Disciplinary Technologies in Educational Psychology

The disciplinary technologies (i.e., hierarchical observation, normalizing judgment, examination) described by Foucault (1977/ 1995) are operative in the discipline of educational psychology's discursive practices. The illustration of these technologies provides a way to interrogate how educational psychology uses power and knowledge to normalize students, i.e., to render students docile, neutral, and appropriate subjects. This interrogation highlights practices of the dominant discourse given expression in classic texts with the hope of "making the familiar strange" (Foucault, 1995). When practices seem strange they are more open to critique and more readily able to be changed.

The technologies of the discipline come together in various practices generated and perpetuated by the discipline of educational psychology. The specific areas to be discussed are:

1. The surveillance practices that pervade educational settings.
2. Classroom management practices.
3. The practice of testing, especially standardized testing.

In using these practices, teachers step into the web of power relations through which students are normalized. Through an uncritical use of these practices teachers participate in their own normalization as well, i.e., they become docile and useful.

Surveillance Practices

In today's educational settings developing the capacity to see students clearly is represented as key to teacher effectiveness. Bentham's panopticon is a metaphor for a characteristic teachers are encouraged to develop, i.e., "withitness." The panopticon was meant to effect "the state of consciousness and permanent visibility that assures the automatic functioning of power" (Foucault, 1995, p. 201). Gage and Berliner (1991) describe a similar effect of withitness: "the knack of seeming to know what is going on all over the room, of having 'eyes in the back of your head.' A teacher's awareness, and the students' awareness of it, makes a difference. Teachers with high withitness make few mistakes in identifying which student is misbehaving, in determining which of two behaviors is the more serious, or in timing an effort to stop a misbehavior" (p. 512).

Woolfolk (1995) also highlights the importance of "withitness" as a characteristic of effective classroom managers whose classes are "relatively free of problems." These are contrasted with ineffective managers whose classrooms are "continually plagued by chaos and disruption" (p. 416). Woolfolk states that withitness "means communicating to students that you are aware of everything that is happening in the classroom, that you aren't missing anything" (p. 416). Woolfolk repeats the optic power image of "eyes in the back of your head" and adds that "withit" teachers

> . . . avoid becoming absorbed or interacting with only a few students, since this encourages the rest of the class to wander. [With-it teachers] are always scanning the room, making eye contact with individual students, so the students know they are being monitored. . . . These teachers prevent minor disruptions from becoming major. They also know who instigated the problem, and they make sure the right people are dealt with. In other words, they do not make . . . timing errors (waiting too long before intervening) or target errors (blaming the wrong student and letting the real perpetrators escape responsibility for their behavior). (pp. 417–419)

"Withit" teachers convey to students that they can be seen and are being monitored continuously. Students know they will be punished for a transgression. An important effect of the proper development of this quality in teachers is so they will be able to "catch" and correct misbehaving students.

The economy of this surveillance technique is a key factor in its utility. Since students know that there is always the possibility that they are being watched, they are encouraged to internalize the gaze of their supervisor learning to monitor themselves and each other. The direction is clear, "Teach students to monitor themselves" (Woolfolk, 1995, p. 420). Thus, the power relations in the classroom are diffused as teachers watch students, students watch teachers, themselves, and each other, and so forth. There is a web of relations of surveillance being weaved as Foucault (1995) insists "from top to bottom . . . bottom to top . . . and laterally" (pp. 176–177).

Classroom Management

Despite the promised effectiveness of surveillance, or because of teachers' ineffective use of surveillance techniques (Gage & Berliner, 1991), children do "misbehave." Classroom management programs and practices are recommended by the mainstream discourse as explicitly aimed at maintaining an atmosphere conducive to learning, yet there is another side to these practices. Management practices are powerful tools (i.e., technologies) used in the normalization of students as they effect increasingly finer differential categories of what it means to "misbehave." The discursive practices of classroom management attend to the finer and finer differentiation of the specific aspects of everyday behavior.

Classroom management is a topic of special and growing import in educational psychology. There has been a marked increase in discussion of this topic in the past few decades, and it has been characterized as the number one concern of classroom teachers (Randolph & Evertson, 1994). According to a report of content analysis of educational psychology textbooks (Ash & Love-Clark, 1985), classroom management increased in amount of actual text space by 75% from 1954–1964 to 1965–1975. There was reported a 100% increase from 1965–1975 to 1976–1983 in text space. The authors of this analysis speculated that the increased discussion might reflect the movement of textbooks toward the more pragmatic concerns of teachers and away from the 'softer' side of educational psychology (Ash & Love-Clark, 1985).[8] Despite their lack of ability to draw definitive conclusions from this descriptive report, the authors state that there have been changes in textbooks used in educational psychology. These changes are reported to be aimed at the practical aspects of classroom life and away from theoretical considerations.

The Woolfolk (1995) text then is representative of this shift in its attentiveness to the importance of issues related to classroom management. Woolfolk (1995) notes that classroom management is "one of the main concerns of teachers, particularly beginning teachers, as well as administrators and parents (p. 401). Woolfolk (1995) cites a Gallup Poll of the public's attitude toward public schools to substantiate this claim. Sixteen of the first seventeen polls list "lack of discipline"[9] as the "number one problem facing schools" (p. 402). Since the late 1980s only "drug use" and "funding" issues have seized first place.

Gage and Berliner (1991), likewise, relate that all classroom needs fall into a "rough order of priority . . . the first [being] the establishment of classroom discipline, control, and management" (p. 509). It is claimed that "without it [classroom discipline, control, and management] nothing much of educational value can be done" (p. 509). Gage and Berliner (1991) also state that the issue of classroom management and discipline is considered by many administrators and teachers to be the "most important cause of teacher failure . . . [and the] leading cause for dismissal" (p. 510). If teachers are judged as being ineffective in their management of classrooms, they can be dismissed. This indicates that the web of power relations in classroom management practice affects teachers and students alike.

There are many points that could be made in a critique of the discourse and practices of educational psychology regarding classroom management. Three areas are particularly problematic. The practices of classroom management are based on a preemptory perspective indicative of hierarchical observation. The questioned of who is "empowered" through management practices needs to be addressed. There is a question of a shift in emphasis from management as a way to access the curriculum to curriculum as a way to ensure good management.

The discursive practices of traditional classroom management come out of a modernist view that the social world is locked into irrationality. Chaos will reign if order is not established and controlled (Ball, 1990). Practices are directed to the "problems" that arise in classrooms. As discussed in chapter 4, these problems are viewed through the perspective of a rationality that looks for technical solutions that can be applied to restore or maintain order. Teachers and educational psychologists define, interpret, and judge both the students who resist the management practices and students' action from a hierarchical position in ways that limit the meanings that the behavior may have.

These judgments are based on an "assumption that there is a proper, correct, standard, or agreed manner of carrying oneself" (Berry, 1995, p. 89). The teacher and educational psychologist know what that proper deportment looks like, and they can easily spot improper behavior. The judgment of proper/improper behavior is based on a "norm" and increasingly fine deviations from the "norm." In such an atmosphere the "non-conformist, even the temporary one, [becomes] the object of disciplinary attention" (Dreyfus & Rabinow, 1983, p. 158). Although the judgments of both students and their actions are always historically, socially, and politically contingent, they are seldom problematized as such.

For example, Woolfolk (1995) recognizes that difference in behavior may have cultural links. The critique that American schools "typically reflect the white, Anglo-Saxon, Protestant, middle-class, male-dominated values that have characterized mainstream America" (p. 155) is accepted as a valid appraisal. Readers are told that schooling formerly was thought to be "the fire under the melting pot" (p. 154). The importance of moving away from this assimilationist perspective, which takes this mainstream perspective as normative, is espoused; a new image of "mosaic" (p. 157) that "celebrates" and values diverse cultural behavior is introduced.[10]

However, the mainstream norm and the deficit orientation model that judges nonmainstream behaviors as inferior resists displacement in the meaning-making basis of the text. Readers are instructed to "teach students directly about how to be students. In the early grades this could mean directly teaching the courtesies and conventions of the classroom: how to get a turn to speak, how and when to interrupt the teacher, how to whisper. . . . You can ask students to learn "how we do it in school" without violating [the] principle . . . respect your students" (Woolfolk, 1995, p. 189). What needs to be highlighted is that while Woolfolk recognizes that "how we do it in school" exhibits the values of the dominant culture and is regarded as problematic, it is never disrupted or displaced. Standards of the Anglo, male, middle-class culture remain the favored paradigm and retain the privileged position. These "standards" become the universal norm that is used to judge behavior as proper or not, and children are judged for their compliance to these norms.

Earlier in the chapter normalizing judgment was discussed as both imposing homogeneity and constructing individuality simultaneously. This dual effect is obvious in classroom management practices as conformity to the homogeneous norm is privileged as the universal standard. Once the norm is established, finer differentiation from the norm can be perceived and measured; eventually individuals can be ranked in relation to each other.

Other examples from Gage and Berliner (1991) explicate the privileged and uninterrogated view of teachers judging the behavior of students from a universalized norm. Activities of students' "misbehavior" are placed in two simple categories: too many unwanted behaviors and too few wanted behaviors. Unwanted behaviors are listed as "physical aggression, moving around the room at inappropriate times, making too much noise, challenging authority at the wrong time or in the wrong way, and making unjust or destructive criticism and complaints" (p. 511). Behaviors that are wanted and need to be increased include "volunteering to recite, standing up for his or her own opinion, paying attention to what is being explained or discussed in class, being involved and active in individual or group projects" (p. 516). What these actions mean to the students themselves is ignored or marginalized as unimportant. Behaviors are simply assigned to one category or another, and the ambiguous nature of students' behavior is eschewed. For instance, a student may view his or her own behavior as "standing up for his or her opinion" (a wanted behavior), while the teacher judges the same action as "challenging authority in the wrong way" or making "unjust criticism." Deeper meanings of student behavior seem unimportant as the focus is on maintaining order and control. More frequently, that which is labeled misbehavior is lack of compliance to the preferred norm. What is ignored is that students are the ones producing the behavior that needs to be managed in the first place (Everhart, 1983). Students give meaning to their behavior.[11]

Everhart (1983) explains that student behavior has social and political contingencies, and these extend beyond the classroom experience. Students, for example, understand their assignment to roles within the classroom and in the broader social context. Their activity forms a subculture as they struggle with the social and political aspects of schooling. As Everhart (1983) explains:

> Classroom management must be understood as a social system, but also as an interface between the state educational system and students. Classroom management mediates social life as students attempt to "make" themselves in a world in which political consciousness, class interests, and cultural regularities enter into the calculus of appropriateness and certitude by which students define themselves. (p. 170)

Students, from a sociopolitical perspective, are viewed as active agents. As such they comply or resign themselves to their assigned roles, or they devise various strategies through which they contest and resist the management practices of teachers and their assignment to low status positions in classrooms and schools.[12] Oppositional behavior of students may well be an appropriate response to an oppressive education (Kohl, 1994). Students have a sense that an oppressive education is preparing and directing them to life in subordinate positions in society. Their minimal involvement in school activities, explicit signs of boredom, or oppositional behavior may signify their own feelings of alienation from the process and product of their work. Through their own oppositional activities students act to reappropriate control of their labor process (Everhart, 1983). In recognizing the sociopolitical aspects of classroom relations, much may be learned by teachers and students alike.

Teachers and students need to learn from students' oppositional activity. Frequently these activities are a mark of student agency; however, they also have a negative impact on students' lives. Perhaps one of the most dramatic forms of oppositional behavior that a student can perform is actually dropping out of school. "Dropping out" is seldom mentioned, questioned, or explored from a sociopolitical perspective in the mainstream discourse of educational psychology. Woolfolk (1995) notes, for example, that in the high school years teachers can focus on academics more than procedures and rules because "[b]y this time, unfortunately, many students with overwhelming behavioral problems have dropped out" (p. 405). The lack of attention supports Fine's (1991) critique that the exodus of students, especially low-income students of color, from high schools "is represented as if it were all quite natural" (p. 8).

Classroom management is generally represented as a way to promote the empowerment of students. Even so, both texts advance models that focus on the empowerment of the teacher-manager (Ball, 1990). Students are not considered in terms of their own learning, agency, desires, and fears as discussed above. In the models presented in the discourse of the classic texts, the focus is on what teachers do to maintain control and compliance; the technical rationality of the discipline is obvious as the activity of the teacher is central.

Gage and Berliner (1991), for example, present classroom

teaching practices in terms of how the teacher gains power in contrast to the students who have none:

> From the teacher's point of view you'll be looking at classroom teaching as an activity in which you have the power to shape the process. You probably had little of that power when you were in the student's role. Then you did pretty much what your teacher wanted you to do. Now, as the teacher, you have the determining role and the responsibility that goes with it. . . . We will introduce you to a diverse set of teaching behaviors that can help you plan and actually be more effective whatever the subject or grade. (p. 494)

In discussing issues of classroom management the perspective of Gage and Berliner (1991) is clearly based in behavioristic psychology. The teacher gains power, and order is maintained through this system set in a discourse of control; management is a case of extinguishing unwanted behavior and increasing wanted behavior. Several strategies are suggested:

> One way of stopping misbehavior is to extinguish it, to withhold reinforcement. This usually means not paying attention to it. . . . Where it is feasible, simply ignore the [misbehaving] student. Turn your back, pay attention to a student who is behaving properly, walk away. . . . Extinction takes time. It may be a while before a child's misbehavior begins to decrease. But be careful. Even an occasional reinforcement on your part can undo the whole process. (p. 513)

This is an example of a traditional prescriptive approach to classroom management in that the focus is directed toward the activities the teacher needs to perform in order to keep students on task and attentive (Everhart, 1983). Educational psychology's purpose is to equip the teacher with techniques through which he or she is more able to control classroom agendas.

Gage and Berliner (1991) recognize that the perspective presented in this text is *traditional* in that it "centers more on the teacher than the student" (p. 492). This perspective is represented as having an advantage over other perspectives of classroom management and teaching (e.g., student-centered instruction, open and humanistic education). The advantage that is reported is that traditional, teacher-centered educational practices have lasted over so many decades; they are "viable." As Gage and Berliner (1991) explain, "it has one important advantage—viability. It is the kind of teaching toward which teachers gravitate and to which they return" (p. 492).

However, it is noted that this perspective and its practices are not entirely in the best interest of students. Gage and Berliner (1991) report the comment of Cuban that this model "has been extremely viable, *for better or worse*" (emphasis added, p. 492). This method of classroom management is accepted as normative and unproblematic despite the expressed possibility that it may not be in the best interest of students.

The practices encouraged in the text manifest a vulgar pragmatism (Cherryholmes, 1988) as the emphasis is focused on what works, regardless of the underside of the effects. What Gage and Berliner (1991) leave out in reference to Cuban's work, and the discussion of classroom management in general, is the reason teacher-centered styles of classroom management persist. Cuban (1984) theorizes that "[s]chools are a form of social control and sorting" (p. 9), echoing the social reproduction and correspondence theory of Bowles and Gintis (1976). Cuban (1984) argues:

> The ways schools are organized, the curriculum, and teaching practices mirror the norms of the socioeconomic system. . . . teacher practices become functional to achieve those ends . . . [i.e.,] reinforcing the teacher's authority to control the behavior of the class. . . . the practices encouraged by student-centered instruction ill-fit the character of the society children will enter and classrooms became inhospitable arenas for small group instruction, expression, student decision making, etc. Teacher-centered instruction, however, endured because it produces *student behaviors expected by the larger society.* (emphasis added, p. 9)

Cuban (1984) has connected the micropractices of schooling with the macrovalues of the larger society. These issues are left unquestioned, even obscured, in the classic educational psychology texts. Through the traditional practices of classroom management students can be normalized, made proper citizens of the state, i.e., docile and useful.

The use of behavioristic psychology, so typical of traditional teacher-centered classroom management practices, exemplifies clearly the "shaping" of students to conform to norms that have become naturalized. What also needs to be noted as well is that humanistic psychologies also are useful in the normalization of students, albeit their role in government is subtler. In student-centered classrooms that espouse humanist psychology the emphasis is on the empowerment of the student. Students are understood as active meaning-makers striving to know themselves and to become self-actualized. Gage and Berliner (1991) explain self-actualized students as: "people who come to accept themselves, their feelings, and others more fully. These people are self-directed, confident, mature, realistic about their goals, and flexible. They've gotten rid of maladjustive behaviors. They become like the people they want to be" (p. 479).

This student-centered perspective seems to be an improvement on the teacher-centered, traditional model. However, while students are perceived as central to the meaning-making system, they are considered self-contained, separate, and isolated from the social and the political contingencies that generate the categories into which they place themselves. Getting rid of "maladjustive behaviors" mentioned in the quote above could be indicative of an even subtler interiorization of a dominant and possibly oppressive norm.

Usher and Edwards (1994) state that humanistic discourses can be more powerful than the objectifying discourses generated by behavioristic psychology. In "subjectifying discourses, within which humanistic psychology has been strongly implicated . . . [d]iscipline is not something externally imposed by teachers since students discipline themselves" (p. 51); it is possible to argue that "regulation works by empowerment" (p. 50). Humanistic psychology, too, provides the "justification and the means for intervention and 'shaping'" (p. 53) students under the illusion of self-governance.

There has been a discernible shift toward the control of students through the use of the curriculum. McNeil (1983) asks readers to picture a one-room schoolhouse of the last century. The students sit on hard benches or at desks in rows facing front; students stand to recite; for much of the day they are silent and still. The teacher or schoolmaster is stern, perhaps wielding a hickory stick. There the purpose for the discipline is *to help the students access the curriculum*. Classroom management and discipline traditionally are viewed as instrumental to the learning of the curriculum.

To a major extent, classroom management procedures of the

current day are much different, although they purportedly are intended for the same purpose, i.e., to help students access the curriculum. Woolfolk (1995) lists more time for learning and greater access to learning as reasons for management practices. Gage and Berliner (1991) insist nothing educational happens without good management practices. However, there is an indication of an obvious shift in the idea of management practices of educational psychology. While classroom management practices are instrumental in helping students access the curriculum, there is also evidence that there is an inversion, i.e., the curriculum is a means of classroom management. For example, Gage and Berliner (1991) connect "misbehavior" of students with the way schools are organized. They note: "behavioral problems . . . [can] stem from the way schools are organized. Sometimes school structure forces students to take courses that are inappropriate for them, that do not allow for their individual needs or level of achievement" (p. 510). They continue to explain that schools that do not allow for students' "individual needs or levels of achievement," as well as a variety of other issues that are outside the teachers' control, contribute to the "crime, delinquency, and problem behavior that exist in [the schools]" (p. 511). The assumption is that the needs of students are met when they are correctly placed in *appropriate* learning groups and given the appropriate information. When students receive their proper educational experience, they will not misbehave. Thus, there is signaled an inversion of means and ends. Where the practices of classroom management were intended as means toward the end of accessing knowledge, there is a shift. The curriculum may also be used as a means through which schools control students.

Testing and the Production of Students

Following Foucault's (1995) position that normalization is a major aspect of the role of schooling, the formation of the "norm" is a key consideration. As presented above, there may be a tacit endorsement by educationalists of what is "normal" or normative based on the commonsense acceptance of certain values, beliefs, and behaviors. These norms are reflective of the preference of the dominant groups and adopted as universal norms by social institutions, schools in particular. Norms grow in power through hegemonic control, i.e., they are validated by meaning-making systems and granted consent by members of subordinate as well as dominant groups. They need to be continually exposed and critiqued. However, there is another area that needs to be highlighted regarding the establishment of norms.

Foucault (1995) has noted the increasingly complex nature of the normalization process in that it has become "possible," through the human sciences, to measure or quantify what is judged to be "normal." The technologies of hierarchical observation and normalizing judgment come together in the quantifying of an evaluative judgment. This is so much of the work of educational psychology exemplified by its emphasis on testing.

That "testing of students is ubiquitous" is a truism. Woolfolk (1995) remarks that "if you have seen the cumulative folders that include testing records for individual students over several years, then you know the many ways students are tested in this country" (p. 528). Hanson (1993) asserts that the testing associated with schooling can begin with examinations toddlers take to enter nursery school, and "that is just the beginning of an endless torrent of tests that will probe every corner of their nature and behavior for the rest of their lives" (p. 1). Gage and Berliner (1991) report that a "reasonable estimate" of teacher time devoted to the testing process is 20% to 30%.

Woolfolk (1995) states: "Measurement is evaluation put in quantitative terms—the numeric *description* of an event or characteristic" (emphasis added, p. 514). Educational psychology advances the understanding that through testing practices that produce these measurements the "truth" about an individual can be known. In other words, testing increases the ability to see and describe students. It is necessary to interrogate this familiar notion. It is argued in the following discussion that testing processes, i.e., forms of examination (especially the norm-referenced variety), are *technologies of differentiation and individualization* that *inscribe* rather than describe students. Examinations are also technologies of power that work to establish hierarchies among students,[13] that are a means of control and a method of domination (Foucault, 1995).

An important issue in the understanding of testing practices is the notion of validity, particularly construct validity. Validity is defined by Woolfolk (1995) as the "degree to which a test measures what it is intended to measure" (p. 525). What is generally avoided in mainstream discussions of construct validity is the social construction of these abstract characteristics. Social constructs are considered and treated "as if" they are "real." This exemplifies the problem of *reification*. However, reification of abstract concepts is imperative in testing practices because only "real" things can be measured. Within the ideology of meritocracy, these "real" characteristics need to be understood as innate properties of individuals, stable over time, and varying in measurement in individuals.

Another important issue regarding testing is that it yields "objective" measurements according to a scale that is metric. The "normal distribution" of students along the bell-shaped curve is critical to this understanding. Although the social construction of the normal or bell-shaped curve has been presented and critiqued,[14] the discursive practice continues to be advanced unproblematically in classic texts of educational psychology. It is presented as "natural" as well as "normal."

For example, Woolfolk (1995) states that the "bell-shaped curve, [is] the most famous frequency distribution because it describes many naturally occurring physical and social phenomena" (p. 519).[15] Gage and Berliner (1991) make the connection as well between physical and social characteristics in stating that "both measures of intelligence and height are normally distributed within any specific age, ethnic, and gender group" (p. 57). The argument is that a "naturally occurring" physical phenomenon (e.g., height) and "naturally occurring" social phenomenon (e.g., intelligence) are normally distributed within a specific population.

These authors construct the illusion that there is a metric scale used to measure both phenomena. However, while there is a standard of measure for height (e.g., feet and inches), only an ordinal system can measure "naturally occurring social phenomena."[16] It is more than an illusion that is created though, as Gage and Berliner (1991) state: "One reason for the popularity of tests is that they give us a quantitative estimate of ability or achievement; they tell *us how much*. In education the attributes that interest us emphasize the abilities and achievements of students—such things as intelligence, creativity, spelling ability, science knowledge, and interest in art" (emphasis added, p. 570).

Mensh and Mensh (1991) refer to the bell-shaped curve as a "particularly mystifying aspect of IQ" (p. 75). Although normal distribution may occur regarding the "metric characteristics of animals such as birth weight in cattle. . . . IQ tests do not possess the characteristics for creating a normal curve" (Mensh & Mensh, 1991, p. 172).[17] Nevertheless, educational psychologists continue to insist that the IQ does possess these metric characteristics.

The bell-shaped curve is an arbitrary and social artifact (Lewontin et al., 1996). Testers create tests so that a bell-shaped curve will appear. This approach preserves the illusion that the "tests measure a real characteristic" (Mensh & Mensh, 1991, p. 76). Intelligence and ability tests "have been composed of items *selected* after trial for observed conformity with the normal distribution. Items that showed little correlation with the overall expectations, or with the previous tests of the kind have been systematically excluded" (Morrison, 1977, quoted in Mensh and Mensh, 1991, p. 76).

Woolfolk (1995) refers to this process in the following explanation of basic concepts in standardized test making: "The test items and instructions have been tried out to make sure *they work* and then rewritten and retested as necessary" (emphasis added, p. 517). What is meant by making sure "they work" is that the tests successfully correlate intelligence or ability scores of students taking the test with the placement of students in the social order (Mensh & Mensh, 1991). That "they work" is an indication of their power to differentiate (Gage & Berliner, 1991).

Gage and Berliner (1991) assert that developers of tests use "the tests' differentiating power as their guide" (p. 51). This differentiating power is further explained:

> Partly because of the way the tests were made, and partly because of the way human intelligence functions, the resulting IQ scores . . . fell into a *normal distribution* (emphasis original) which has the bell shape. . . . Why do IQ tests tend to be normally distributed? *Is it simply because the test is rigged? Not entirely* (emphasis added). Remember that the tests consist of many items, each designed to differentiate among individuals. That is, the items are written so that on some items only about half of a given age group responds correctly, while on other items a higher or lower percentage of that group responds correctly. (p. 56)

The standard on which the tests' differentiating power is based is middle-class knowledge. Gage and Berliner (1991) recognize this and give many examples of this bias, and then they excuse it; bias is renamed "relevance":

Middle-class bias has proved much more difficult to eliminate than was anticipated. For tests of intellectual abilities useful in modern American society, a "middle-class" and "urban" orientation may constitute not bias but *relevance*. . . . So we may not want to change the tests so much as we might want to change the environments that promote low test performance. (emphasis added, p. 90)

The suggestion of changing environments as a way to ameliorate low-test scores is contradictory and seems disingenuous. It is contradictory in that "intelligence" is repeatedly represented in the same text as an innate, stable, and inherited characteristic (Gage & Berliner, 1991). How can it improve with a change in environment? It seems disingenuous in that standardized tests *are constructed* to rank a certain percentage of students below the normal range. Effective standardized tests are guaranteed, or, to use Gage and Berliner's term, "rigged" to separate and sort children. This is the differentiating power that guides the development of the tests in the first place. This is how *they work*, why they were developed, and why test questions have to be written and rewritten.

The "differentiating power" of tests is central to their use in educational institutions. The particular "norm" around which they are organized is never made problematic. On the contrary, the middle-class "relevance" is accepted as normative. Award or violence is distributed to students according to their scores or their "marks." Lewontin et al. (1996) explain succinctly:

> . . . the power of the "norm," once established, is that it is used to judge individuals who have been located along its linear scale. Deviations from the norm are regarded with alarm. Parents who are told that their child is two standard deviations from the norm on some behavioral scale are led to believe that he or she is "abnormal" and should be adjusted in some way to psychometry's Procrustean bed. Psychometry, above all, is a tool of a conformist society that, for all its professed concern with individuals, is in reality mainly concerned to match them against others and to attempt to adjust them to conformity. (p. 149)

Norms are established by validating *what works* in differentiating those considered "normal" from those who are not. The argument is circular. The process of standardized testing establishes what is "normal" based on information gathered on those who are considered normal. The deficit view of those outside this norm is a form of "popular racism" (Rizvi, 1993).

Although the classic texts never say exactly who the norming sample is, it is noted that "social class, race, gender, and ethnicity can be relevant considerations" (Gage & Berliner, 1991, p. 574) if there is a concern with equal opportunity. It is stated that there is a "problem that many African American, Chicanos, and Native Americans face with norm referenced testing when the norms are based on distant but supposedly representative, peer groups" (Gage & Berliner, 1991, p. 574). When this information is added to the "problem" that a hypothetical student named "Lisa" is having with her national percentile rank, then all the clues point to the norm group. The norm group is male, Anglo, and middle class. It is important to note that although Gage and Berliner (1991) regard social class, race, and gender to be "relevant" considerations in discussions of equality, these same characteristics become "irrelevant" when the interest is in selecting "highly competent rather than mediocre" (p. 574) students.

The "objective" evaluation of students according to scores produced through testing needs to be regarded as a process that produces normalcy. This process also describes deviance from the norm. As more tests are taken by students, their cumulative folder expands, and "more knowledge leads to more specification" (Dreyfus & Rabinow, 1983, p. 159). There is developed a new visibility and a more minute describability. The "examination is at the center of the procedures that constitute the individual as both effect and object of power, as effect and object of knowledge" (Foucault, 1995, p. 192).

There is a certain "alchemy" in this process. The properties of a discipline's regime, i.e., its norms, values, procedures, become attributes of persons. Rose (1989) expresses this well:

> The procedures of visualization, individualization and inscription that characterize the mental sciences reverse the direction and domination between human individuals and the scientific and technical imagination. They domesticate and discipline subjectivity, transforming the intangible, changeable, apparently free-willed conduct of people into manipulable, coded, materialized, mathematized, two-dimensional traces which may be utilized in any procedure of calculation. The human individual has become calculable and manageable. (p. 129)

Disciplines are ways of naming and ordering differences. Through their testing procedures, they allow educators to categorize all the complexity students by reducing them to scores that can be illustrated on graphs and tables. The result of testing practices has profound effects on lives of students. Gage and Berliner (1991) remind us: "All your life you've been taking tests. They have brought you success or failure, joy or sorrow, a sense of justice done or outrage suffered" (p. 569). That there is not more outrage attests to the hegemonic control this disciplinary practice of educational psychology exerts.

This chapter is entitled *Disciplining the Discipline* in order to highlight the activity of placing the discursive practices of the discipline under scrutiny. Utilizing the process of critical reading and Foucault's methods of critique, it is possible to look at the modern science of educational psychology differently. The practices of the discipline, its disciplinary technologies, are usually considered progressive. In other words, they are considered a means of enabling students, i.e., practices are used in the liberatory interest of education. However, the limits of these technologies need to be recognized as they are utilized to judge, construct, and normalize students as subjects of a particular kind, docile and useful.

The questioning of the discipline's practices is not aimed at looking for answers or universal solutions. Rather, questioning is regarded as a way to engage the issues of the discipline more deeply and complexly. Questioning indicates a desire to interrogate "what what we do does" in the real-life experiences of children so that we can think about students and our own practice differently. A critique of the discipline needs to become an important part of the disciplinary practice.

CHAPTER 6

PRAXIS

[H]ow do we relate our ideas and values to our own action? Everything
we affirm and defend . . . must find expression in relevant action. . . . I
believe that revolution begins precisely with revolution in our daily lives.
(Freire & Faundez, 1992, pp. 24–25)

Only through praxis—reflection and action dialectically interacting to
re-create our perception and description of reality—can people become
subjects in control and organizing their society.
(Frankensteine & Powell, 1994, p. 76)

The text containing the Freire and Faundez quote above is ex-
horting us to give expression through our actions to our ideas and
values. The authors point out the very real possibility that there
are often gaps between our beliefs and our actions. In a sense we
are revolutionaries in that we understand things (e.g., our situations, disciplines, values) in ways that push against mainstream,
accepted, and often oppressive rationalities. However, as Freire
and Faundez (1992) go on to explain, we are revolutionaries in
the "abstract" only if, when it comes to action, as in teaching,
we fall into or continue along our usual and ordinary ways.

I appreciate this exhortation of Freire and Faundez (1992) as I
increasingly asked myself how I can give clear expression to my
beliefs through pedagogy. My practice as a teacher has and is continually undergoing transformation because I could not possibility continue to teach educational psychology from a positivist
worldview, i.e., in a way that transmits the objective, scientific
truth and "promise" of the discipline. How could I teach in a way
that fails to recognize the political and culturally hegemonic
"underside" I have been critiquing? How could I continue as
though nothing had happened to me, to my consciousness, to my
way of thinking? At the same time, there are multiple constraints

against reforming my practice, including institutional expectations. Furthermore, mandated external standardized testing practices privilege the static "objective" knowledge of the discipline. Students also present resistance at times, especially when they fail to look at things with an open mind and a willingness to see multiple viewpoints.

The use of the word *revolutionary* may seem dramatic to some, but I think it is an apt descriptor. When practice changes as we contest and resist oppressive, albeit commonsense, discourses we are engaging in political activity as both Foucault and Freire so often point out. This resistance becomes political struggle as efforts to disrupt the status quo often are. The political struggle is based on the idea of solidarity with persons who have been marginalized and is dedicated to a politics of change (Kincheloe, Steinberg, & Villaverde, 1999). The changes being sought are toward a more democratic and emancipatory educational experience for all students.

Very much connected to this struggle is the issue of the "status of truth and the role it plays in how things are done at school" (Smart, 1985, p. 68). At times we need courage to move against the socially constructed and accepted notions of "truth" that create the norm we take for granted. Often the courage we need is nurtured in community, a common unity. This community then becomes a new discursive community.

Praxis is the dynamic concept/construct that expresses the dialectical synthesis of reflection and action. Moacir Gadotti (1994) explains Freire's use of the term, "Praxis is the unity that should exist between what one does (practice) and what one thinks about what one does (theory)" (p. 166). Freire (1992) warns us that either action or reflection alone is merely activism or verbalism, neither of which supports transformation. As I internalize this dynamic of reflection and action and take praxis seriously, my practice of teaching changes.

In this chapter I offer some examples of how the ideas in the preceding chapters, how this way of thinking, has affected my own practice. The issues of praxis I present here are meant to be illustrative rather than some universal formula. It is an example of key concepts that have affected me as I have taken up the work of being a teacher of educational psychology in my own specific location. It is open to constant examination, critique, and revision. Of course, we always need to be critical of our own discourse as well as those of others. Our own discourses demand the reflexivity of critical educators because we are caught in regimes of truth as surely as those whose discourses we critique are. I examine my own discourses and the practices they sanction to better understand "my own involvement in those regimes, and in so doing, I will attempt to find weak spots in them" (Gore, 1993, p. 139). In finding the weak spots in my own practice and reforming them, I can move toward a more liberating experience for my students.

I am self-conscious here in that I recognize that I generally have classes under thirty-five students. I understand that this class size makes a difference in my work. When I was in a discussion group on the Internet a couple of years ago, we were discussing teaching educational psychology. Although I viewed my conversation partners only through the written word, the laughter of some of my colleagues in larger schools was palpable as I "voiced" issues of practice. In many institutions typical class size for educational psychology is twice or three times that of my small class "luxury." The number of students in our classes often catches us between our theories and the reality of our situations. This need not consign us as teachers to the position of "abstract" revolutionaries; rather it does take some creativity to resist being caught in the traditional positivist model of education aimed at the transmission of static knowledge.

Initiating the Process: Becoming Aware

As I mentioned earlier, this work began with an uneasy reading of the discourse of educational psychology as I was teaching introductory courses to preservice teachers. I came to recognize myself in my teaching, in Freire's (1990) terms, as both oppressed and oppressor. I saw myself as oppressed because I had internalized the rationale of the master narrative of the discipline; I had assented to its hegemonic discourse with its power to control, to name, to rank, and to define persons as "objects" through disciplinary technologies, i.e., hierarchical observation, normalizing gaze, examination. It seems as though I myself had been normalized and domesticated, made fit for the educational system, i.e., docile and useful.

I took on the role of the oppressor by teaching the discipline as a neutral body of knowledge and skills. I had been enculturated into its meaning-making system, adopting the perceptions, judgments, and techniques of the discipline. I was critical and reflective in my teaching, but from a position *within* the meaning-making system of the discipline. My intent was to initiate and "train" preservice teachers in the rationality and language of educational psychology. In a sense, I was complicitous in the system of domination (Foucault, 1995). I engaged a process whereby my students would be normalized, and where they, in turn, would learn to direct a normalizing gaze toward their own students using the knowledge, skills, and techniques of the discipline.

Freire's (1992) metaphor of the "banking" concept of education explains this traditional practice well: "Education . . . becomes an act of depositing, in which the students are the depositories and the teacher is the depositor. Instead of communicating, the teacher issues the communiqués and makes deposits which the students patiently receive, memorize, and repeat" (p. 58). A shift in my perspective and consequently my practice took place as I came to experience several *interrelated* processes. I stress *interrelated* because these processes are actually impossible to separate as they occur simultaneously. The first is the understanding and critiquing of knowledge as the result of social activity; knowledge is a social construction. Another process is recognizing discourse as a site of social struggle. The discourse of the discipline is never disinterested; privileged discourses express the knowledge, values, and beliefs of a particular social group just as surely as subaltern discourses do. A third process is intertextual reading. Texts need to be read against other texts because they are embedded in historical, political, and social contexts; in these contexts the beliefs and values expressed through the discourse make sense. Through these interrelated processes I was able to exchange the normalizing gaze of the discipline with a critical gaze, to look back at the disciple's discourse and see things differently (Gallagher, 1999).

Examining Knowledge as a Social Construction

A major concern of this book is how the "truth" of the discipline is constituted. In fact, my own perspective is a social constructionist one. As I have stated throughout this book, I understand all knowledge, including scientific knowledge, to be the result of social processes. The knowledge of the discipline is not so much "discovered" as it is "produced" by real people who have histories, biases, share membership in discursive communities, and are embedded in power relations. Thus, the so-called "truth" of the discipline is the product of social negotiations of the educational psychology community.

The acceptance of a social constructionist perspective within the educational psychology community itself is gaining legitimacy. This viewpoint is espoused as *the* "contemporary psychological perspective" of the educational psychologists (Anderson et al., 1995). As Anderson et al. (1995) propose, "the heart of a contemporary psychological perspective is an image of learners as active and social constructors of meaning, and an image of learning as an act of construction through social interaction in many contexts" (p. 145). The acknowledgment of learning and knowledge as socially constructed is by no means a new development as many concerned with learning have been discussing it for years (e.g., Derry, 1992; Goodenow, 1992; Mayer, 1992; Mead, 1934; Prawat & Floden, 1994; Resnick, Levine, & Teasley, 1991; Scarr, 1985). Indeed, Prawat and Floden (1994) remind us that "[constructionist] learning is based on the now *commonplace* idea that knowledge is actively constructed by the learner" (emphasis added, p. 37).

This perspective exemplifies the disposition encouraged for classroom teachers that can and must be applied to understanding the formation of disciplinary knowledge as well. Unless this position is taken seriously as applying to the knowledge of the discipline, it remains a static "fact" of learning that is told to preservice teachers, while the discipline, as we know it, remains unchanged (Doyle & Carter, 1996). If a social constructionist perspective is taken seriously by those involved with the discipline, there are far-reaching implications for the discipline's knowledge claims. This perspective suggests recognition of the social, cultural, ideological, and political significance of what is said and done in the name of the discipline.

Situated Knowledge

The understanding that all knowledge is fashioned through the interaction of persons in particular socially situated positions with interests and biases is central to a constructionist perspective. Situated knowledge is understood as always partial, shifting, and even distorted. To the modern worldview, with its goal of certainty, this may be regarded as a negative position. However, I regard the claim of a partial vision to be a strength in that it is open and initiates, rather than closes off communication among alternative perspectives (Haraway, 1991).

Those who profess that only situated knowledge is possible claim responsibility for the knowledge they construct. They recognize the importance of learning "to see . . . from another point of view" (Haraway, 1991, p. 190). They understand that there are always multiple points of view, each complex and related to the positionality of the knower. Reflexivity is desired as there is a recognition of personal embeddedness in macrotendencies (Harding, 1991) of society, i.e., the values, meaning-making systems, power relations of one's social world. Contrastingly, the possibility that knowledge could be "objective" or "disinterested" eliminates knowledge construction as a social and cultural activity, and it exempts its constructors from responsibility for its contents and/or effects. From a position of situated knowledge, the claim of neutrality is considered an illusion at best, or a "cloak" at worst, that covers the vested interest of those who get to speak for the discipline, i.e. the experts or the "elite" of the discipline. Positions of power and privilege are protected as the particular worldview of "authorities" is imposed as universal, natural, and normal.

An effect of realizing that all knowledge is situated is that it makes communication among perspectives primary. Sharon Welch (1990) describes "communicative ethics" as combining pluralism and social responsibility. Welch (1990) explains the difference of an "ethic of control," i.e., *power over*, and an "ethic of risk," i.e., *power with*. The ethic of power over issues dictates of truth put the world in order, whereas the "ethic of risk" understands the need for ethical conversations. The goal is "mutual critique leading to a more adequate understanding of what is just and how particular forms of justice may be achieved" (p. 129).

An understanding of the discipline's knowledge claims as situated, partial, and shifting calls for a more reflexive stance from educational psychologists. Recognition of situated knowledges also encourages ethical conversations among those with varied perspectives concerned with the educational enterprise. Too often persons discuss with those who share their position and fail to engage those with differing positions. However, a source of great encouragement is the increase of sessions at professional conferences and journals where multiple positions around a variety of topics are presented and debated. Providing our students with this kind of experience continues to be a challenge.

Students are able to appreciate situated knowledge as they read intertextually, which is discussed below. Students then can create/imagine conversations between and among persons with differing viewpoints. Students are able to craft arguments from multiple theoretical positions and question and debate each other from these positions. Through this kind of activity students seek to understand the rationale of the positions, how arguments are framed within positions, the assumptions that underpin the viewpoint, and how to question and critique. This is much more rigorous work than the focus of arriving at a single correct answer to a situation.

A place of clear explication of situated knowledges, for example, is a topic typically at the center of educational psychology courses, i.e., learning theory. In what milieu do behavioral, cognitive, constructivist theories, for example, make sense? How did the cultural and political embeddedness of Skinner, Piaget, and Vygotsky lead these figures to understand learning as they did? How do various learning theories portend various notions of the student, the teacher, and the teaching-learning experience? The growing influence of Vygotsky even within mainstream discourse opens spaces where this understanding of social, cultural, political embeddedness of teaching-learning is essential.

When discussion and debate are constitutive of the teaching-learning process, students understand more clearly that ideas and people are complex and not simply "right" or "wrong." Students can do this work. Effective discussion and debate are not easy approaches to classroom learning and process. Sometimes students resist the self-conscious critique that results; it can be disconcerting when long-held beliefs lose the potential to help us make sense of the world or are seen as one possibility among many. I accept the resistance but encourage the work nonetheless. Student comments on course evaluations are so telling, e.g., "I am really angry because this course made me rethink and evaluate my ideas"; "I was able to re-evaluate many of my beliefs and I feel I am a better person and a better teacher."

Discourse and Its Productive Activity

Recognizing the discipline's mainstream talk and texts as "discourse" may be a new idea to students, which needs some introduction. The idea of discourse becomes more discernible as multiple and conflicting discourses are introduced. A key point is that the mainstream discourse of the discipline is so powerful in informing how we think about students, teachers, and the teaching-learning process that it needs to be made problematic and critiqued.

Discourse is recognized as a social artifact, the result of social negotiation. Discourse is also the process through which human persons are constituted. This perspective subscribes to the understanding that much of what we have taken as "real" is imminently tied with our use of language. Therefore, the human person as object/subject[1] is understood as *inscribed* by language rather than simply *described* through the objective reporting of the result of scientific research (Gallagher, 1999).

This productive aspect of discourse is a matter that needs to be emphasized continually because the socially produced knowledges of discourses are never neutral. Knowledge claims of discourses work in favor of some people over others. Therefore, discourses are recognized as sites of social struggle. The mainstream discourse regarding classroom management discussed in chapter 5 provides a good example. "Misbehavior," or lack of compliance to a preferred norm or mode of behavior, is a judgment made by the teacher from a specific position and set of interests. The normalizing gaze of the teacher discussed in chapter 5 is operative here. When the same behavior is viewed from another position (e.g., the student's), an alternative discourse is discernible. "Insubordinate" students may be resisting and contesting their social and political positions within the classroom, school, or in current societal arrangements. In other venues or from different positions the same behavior may be represented as "assertive" and considered positive.

A student once shared a personal story with the class that exemplifies this situation. Her teacher was presenting a lesson about Native Americans. The student had firsthand knowledge of Native Americans since her father belonged to a particular group of Native American people, had lived on a reservation, attended an "American" school, and had shared much with his daughter about his life and culture. The student objected to what she considered narrow and stereotypical material that was being taught to the class. When the student's objections were belittled, she did not back down from her objections or become silent. The teacher represented her behavior as "insubordinate," which in a sense it was as she refused to submit to the authority of the teacher. However, as her behavior, which continued through the rest of the course, was judged without the benefit of understanding the complexities of its presentation, she was indeed mislabeled and the teacher recommended her to a class for "behaviorally disturbed" students. This category did not describe any "real" characteristic about the student. However, she was placed in this category and received a very different educational experience as a result. It was evident that even several years after this incident took place, this student was still feeling the effects of being misrepresented and constructed as a particular kind of student.

What I attempt to show in this work, as well as in my teaching, is that the discourse of educational psychology is a site of social struggle. It is powerful in the multiple ways it constructs and differentiates students. If the "insubordinate" student in the scenario related above had accepted the authority of the teacher and perhaps assented to the preferred knowledge of the teacher, she may have been labeled differently, i.e., cooperative, intelligent, "good."

Intertextual Reading and Critical Literacy

The mainstream discourse is also vulnerable to counterdiscourses. These alternative discourses question, resist, and contest the assumptions and knowledge claims of the dominant discourse. The counterdiscourses, are the heteroglossia (Bakhtin, 1981; Lashgari, 1995) discussed in chapter 2. This "talking back" disrupts the definition of the "truth" of the dominant discourse. Foucault's genealogies direct attention to those records of resistance that have not gained acceptance within the mainstream discourse. Genealogies attend to subaltern perspectives and knowledges, opening up a space where knowledge that has been silenced or marginalized can be heard and taken seriously.[2] The dialogic (Lashgari, 1995) that results when these perspectives are taken seriously is necessary in order to ensure a critical literacy regarding educational psychology.

In chapter 3 I discuss the importance of reading intertextually, and throughout chapters 4 and 5 I use this activity to critique the dominant discourse of the discipline. Texts considered outside the mainstream discourse disrupt and subvert the productive power of the mainstream texts. What is highlighted is the power–knowledge nexus of the discourse. Why is one perspective privileged over another in the discipline? Why do the confusing and mistaken representations of issues like "race" or narrow discussions of complex constructs like the examples of "intelligence" offered in chapters 4 and 5 prevail in mainstream discussions? Intertextual reading is a key activity in my own practice as a teacher of educational psychology.

Therefore, choosing texts for educational psychology courses is an important task, as it is for any course. In my classes, the dominant discourse available in educational psychology textbooks is taken seriously. To repeat a recurring theme, the mainstream discourse cannot be ignored as it is so powerful and has had so much influence on the educational experience of our students. Students need to have access to these texts. Usually my students are invited to obtain temporary use of textbooks from my own collection, use texts on reserve at the library, or borrow texts from the library's collection. I have given up requiring students to purchase these textbooks for multiple reasons. One important consideration has been that my students have shared with me their frustration in spending so much money on the book and then to find so much problematic material in them.

Alternative texts are used to present questions and to disrupt the sometimes unconscious assumptions, "neutrality," and smooth historical "development" of educational psychology. Voices or perspectives that pose questions need not be considered "spoilers" to the discipline, as though all was well before their arrival. Rather, alternative perspectives and interrogations can be seen as opportunities to consider the discipline more critically. Recognition of alternative texts focuses on the greater social and political complexity of education as well as educational psychology's implication in social and political contexts. Intertextual reading is necessary if students of educational psychology are to move beyond a functional literacy toward a critical literacy concerning the discipline.

Some important examples of counterdiscourses that facilitate reading against the mainstream texts have already been presented in this book. The feminist critique of science (chapter 2), for example, troubles some of the myths that have been perpetuated regarding neutrality, objectivity, and the primacy of a positivist epistemology. Issues of positionality, vision, and voice point to the reality of situated knowledges. How does this critique of science help us to understand the modern science of educational psychology? Giroux's (1981, 1988) and Kincheloe's (1993) critiques of technical rationality, the dominant meaning-making system of the discipline, assist us in understanding the structure of the discipline. It then becomes possible to see how this structure supports the discipline and also constrains thinking within the discipline.

It is helpful for students to read the material in the textbook regarding classroom management against, for example, Everhart's (1983) discussion and critique of these mainstream models as prescriptive programs. Everhart's recommendation of a sociopolitical understanding of classroom life discussed in chapter 5 contrasts well with the technical view of classroom management presented in mainstream texts. The explication of Mensh and Mensh (1991) concerning the historical development of the psychometric notion of intelligence and the fabrication of the bell-shaped or "normal" curve contradicts the unproblematic explanation of "measuring" intelligence offered in the textbooks.

Students can be confused by these discrepancies. My attention to their confusion is critical. I don't just tell them, "Well, the textbook is wrong, believe this other reading." Rather, together we analyze the readings, deconstruct the codes in each, ask questions regarding who benefits and who is penalized by the position supported in the readings. Students can understand what/whose knowledge has been privileged by the discipline and begin to analyze how/why each makes sense from within a particular worldview. Students are quite able to evaluate the implications and ramifications of various readings for the teaching-learning experience.

I am self-conscious here in that I choose the texts for a course. I am presenting what I have come to see as important. I am open to the possibility that students may not see the importance of these texts. I encourage students to bring in other texts or issues found in student research, media presentations, in movies, music, and most directly in their own experience.

Students' Experiences as Text

I always tell students that so much of learning begins with their own experiences—although learning cannot end there. Even though they are frequently overlooked or disregarded, students' own experiences of schooling are a valuable source of discussion and knowledge production in educational psychology. In fact, Dewey (1938) has pointed out that there is an organic connection between experience and education. Nevertheless, often the content and process of educational psychology and students' experiences fail to connect (Kincheloe & Steinberg, 1999) in traditional classes.

Students' experiences can be considered "texts" that need to be read, analyzed, and critiqued. Our students are experts in the field of educational psychology. As I assure them of their expertise I notice their surprised, questioning, and sometimes nervous looks. They have experienced twelve or more years of schooling, and I encourage them that they probably have learned their lessons in educational psychology very well. They may not have acquired the formal language of the discipline, but they all have experienced (some have suffered) its effects. They are experts in the sense that they have internalized the meaning and accepted the practices promulgated by the discourse. Their bodies have been disciplined by the discipline, made docile and useful (Foucault, 1995), or, as Freire (1992) would say, they have been "domesticated" through their schooling experience.

I understand domestication as a vulgar form of socialization, akin to Foucault's sense of normalization. Students are rationalized as adaptable, as able to be "trained" so as to live in particular cultural, political, and economic milieus as useful citizens. For some students, especially those who do not fit the idealized norm, their becoming acceptable has come at a high personal cost. Whereas while many students have learned to play the game of domestication through schooling, they often have not given assent to the oppressive proclivities of its regime.

Students have numerous and varied stories to tell regarding their experiences of schooling. Sometimes they are tales of success and how the system supported their desires and talents. The stories students often tell with the most enthusiasm are connected with their subversion of the system, how they beat the system or used the system to their own advantage. I connect these stories to the students' refusal to be domesticated. Foucault encourages us to look for the tiny eruptions, places of resistance, contestation, and potential engagement. These eruptions are signs of our educational system's attempts to regulate and control students. They can be understood as glimpses into the oppressive characteristics of schooling if we take these signs seriously and believe they have something to tell us, and/or if we believe the students have something to tell us.

As discussed above, student behavior that moves against an established and acceptable norm, while possibly considered a sign of agency of the student, does not always produce positive effects. Students receive labels, punishments, rewards, differential treatment, and so forth, according to their behavior or performance. The consequences of actions can be painful as the story related by my student who was Native American. Students tell these stories, too. Similar accounts can be found in numerous alternative texts (e.g., Kohl, 1994; Weis & Fine, 1993; Willis, 1977). However, when possible and available, I use the texts of my students' experiences. The mainstream discourse in textbooks and student produced texts can be read intertextually.

Foregrounding Contexts

A significant ramification of this mode of analysis is an interest in displaying the contextual embeddedness of any discourse. For example the historical formation of the discipline and/or constructs of the discipline, including the social actors and the various cultural and political milieus in which the discipline is embedded, are important in understanding how and why the discipline developed as it did. This approach represents a significant shift for the discipline.

The discipline of educational psychology is presented in classic texts as ahistorical. There are few references to historical contexts or figures[3] in texts. A synchronic aspect of the discipline is indicated in that its focus is one moment in time, like a snapshot (Cherryholmes, 1988). This situation is typical of a positivist epistemology, but it also has been taken to imply an "apparent lack of interest in the history of [the] field" (Glover & Ronning, 1987, p. vii). This apparent lack of interest in the history of the discipline is supported by mainstream prescriptions for introductory classes. Anderson et al. (1995) specifically contend that preservice teachers do not need to understand the history of psychological ideas. The importance of understanding the history of the field is reserved for educational psychologists.

Despite this lack of consideration for the historical development of the discipline, Sandra Harding (1991), philosopher of science, asserts that there may be serious reasons why the history of science is not taught to newcomers to the discipline. Harding wonders if there is a fear that students would feel the enterprise is not worth the effort if they knew the history. She asks: "What should we want students to know about the scientific enterprise, its history, practices, and goals? Would any of them go through the arduous training necessary to become a scientist [or educational psychologist] if they were told the truth, the whole truth, and nothing but the truth about this institution and its present-day practices?" (p. 31).

To include the history of the discipline may well turn our students against some constructs of the discipline or, at least, give them an appreciation of the contexts in which the discipline has developed as it has. It may be "risky" to include this material, but there is a greater risk in not including historical information. Historical material regarding the discipline certainly highlights the social construction of its knowledge base and thereby allows for the cultivation of a critical literacy of the discipline.

The example of Francis Galton provides a helpful illustration. What would students of educational psychology think about some of the discipline's central issues (e.g., dualistic nature-nurture questions, psychometric testing) if they knew about the context and person who initiated them, namely, Francis Galton (1822–1911). Galton is described as "a strong influence on what became American psychology . . . who was not a psychologist at all, but a wealthy and somewhat eccentric Briton" (Glover & Ronning, 1987, p. 19).

I always include in my own presentation or through student research attention to Galton's historical context in presenting the concepts he found meaningful and the ideas he advanced. The second half of the nineteenth century was a time of social unrest in many areas of the world. In Galton's England the "increasing urbanization brought about by rapid industrialization produced the appalling conditions of the Victorian slums" (Burman, 1994, p. 13). In upper-class circles this situation created anxiety regarding the quality of the "stock" gathered around industrial sites. The specific focus was on those seen as "unstable and unruly" and consequently considered a threat to the social order (Burman, 1994).

Galton's thinking was organized around a hereditarian view of personal qualities, and he "pursued interests that led to the field of eugenics" (Glover & Ronning, 1987, p. 19). In fact, Galton is considered the "father" of the eugenics movement (Fancher, 1979). The idea of "ideological inheritance" (Kincheloe & Steinberg, 1993) is helpful here. Galton's assumptions and practices had a great influence on many educational psychologists who were to follow in his footsteps, including J. McKeen Cattell, Edward E. Thorndike, and Lewis M. Terman. Galton provided a foundation for many who would influence the development of the discipline of educational psychology with its practical concerns for the classification, measurement, and eventual "betterment" (read regulation) of populations of school children.

Even today Galton "remains a central figure in the progress of modern psychology" (Fancher, 1979, p. 294). Even so, when Galton is mentioned, albeit in passing, in classic texts (e.g., Gage & Berliner, 1991), his position is unproblematic and seemingly neutral. Nevertheless, his ideas connected to eugenics can be found throughout the text and talk of mainstream educational psychology. When students know Galton's position concerning eugenics they read texts differently. Ideas connected to the eugenics movement provide a subtext in the following excerpt from the Gage and Berliner (1991) textbook, found in the section on gifted and talented students:

> Galton . . . published the first study of people reported to be geniuses in 1869. Later interest in giftedness was strengthened by advances in the measurement in intelligence. . . . A major milestone in the field was reached when Lewis M. Terman . . . initiated a longitudinal study of approximately fifteen hundred gifted students. . . . [which] helped disprove many misconceptions about gifted people. As a group they are equal to or better than average in physical stature and health, popularity and social acceptance, emotional health and freedom from behavioral disorders. They also maintain or increase their intellectual ability and productivity as they grow older. (p. 216)

So much of the discipline's legacy can be traced to Galton. His influence does matter. Even so, this influence has remained unexamined and is rarely mentioned, let alone critiqued, in most educational psychology discourse.

Knowing the historical background provides us with a whole new area of insight into the development of the discipline and its legacy. Sorting, measuring, ordering students have been among the constant practices of educational psychology. Educational psychologists subscribe to these practices so that we might "better serve" students in spite of the clear deleterious effects on some students. Robert V. Guthrie (1976) included a chapter in his book, *Even the Rat Was White: A Historical View of Psychology,* that he entitled "The Past Is Prologue." It is distressing to read his reflections of more than twenty years ago:

> Some of the dubious research of the 1920's has lingered nearly fifty years as a phantomlike apparition of pseudointellectualism. Present-day proclamations . . . resemble the claims of biased 1920 educational psychologists. . . . These theories recur with an appearance of "newness" enough to obscure the cobwebs of antiquity and actually encourage a repeat of the same defenses utilized decades ago. This is occurring today in the arguments against the continued use of IQ tests and the allegations of inherited mental deficits in black and brown children. (p. 194)

That "not that much has changed" in the ensuing twenty years is evidenced in the publication of *The Bell Curve* (Herrnstein & Murray, 1994). The discourse of educational psychology and its practices support and construct the conditions that made Guthrie's statement meaningful in the 1970s and give his words meaning today. Unless educational psychologists examine the legacy of their discipline, this quote will be current twenty years from now as well.

Students need a comprehensive understanding, a critical literacy, of the discipline that includes an examination of its historical formation. Foucault (1988) insists that the difference between a "real" science and a pseudo-science is that a real science "recognizes and accepts its own history without feeling attacked" (p. 12). Facing the history of a modern science may be disruptive to champions of a discipline like educational psychology, especially when the history exposes undeniable propensities toward racism, sexism, and classism. What results from a failure to confront this history is "social amnesia" (Giroux, 1981) as the memory of the past has been concealed or silenced in the interest of advancing disciplinary programs. Failure to confront the social, historical, political contexts of the discipline promotes an insidious "scientific illiteracy" (Harding, 1991) regarding the formation of the discipline's discourse and its sanctioned practices that pervade the educational system in this country.

Our own discourses have contexts in which they are embedded as well. Our beliefs, values, meaning-making systems, and so forth, or as Kincheloe and Steinberg (1993) describe our "ideological inheritance," have social, cultural, political, economic influences. In other words, the way we come to think about ourselves, the world and our place in it, the teaching-learning process, and knowledge and "truth" do not arise in us naturally or are arrived at scientifically, but are the result of a myriad of influences. So frequently we, students and teachers, remain unaware of these influences, which, while they support our worldview, also constrain it. As critical educators we have the responsibility to examine our "ideological inheritance" and to open spaces where our students can also. Kincheloe and Steinberg (1993) say it well:

> Our conception of self and the world . . . can only become critical when we appreciate the historicity of its formation. We are never independent of the social and historical forces that surround us—we are all caught at a particular point in the web of reality. [Our] project is to understand what that point in the web is, how it constructs our vantage point, and the ways it insidiously restricts our vision. (p. 302)

Students need opportunities to grapple with the influences of their own "point in the web of reality" and how it influences their worldview. This is always *possible* in a class where teacher-talk predominates, as students are active in their own learning. However, it is not *probable*, as students are busy taking notes or dreaming of ways to escape boredom. Lecture, teacher-directed questions, one-way flow of information so indicative of a positivist epistemology rarely results in examination of worldview.

The grappling with such issues requires an experience rich in dialogue. Dialogue is one of those words people use frequently and yet has very different meanings. As Paulo Freire (1992) explains, dialogue is an *encounter* between persons. Used in this way, dialogue "cannot be reduced to the act of 'depositing' ideas in another, nor can it become a simple exchange of ideas to be consumed by the discussants. Nor yet is it a hostile, polemical argument between [persons] who are committed . . . to the imposition of *their* truth" (emphasis added, p. 77). Although some disagreements can occur, the encounters described by Freire are not marked by hostility. They are characterized by an infusion of love, faith in and commitment to others, humility, and mutual trust. In this encounter all are transformed—teacher and student, our action, and the world. Students do not have to think the way I do or the way the other students do; the requirement is that everyone takes the material of the class and each other seriously.

Understanding dialogue in this way does not mean that the teacher abdicates responsibility for the learning of the class, does not have authority, or is not a resource for students. However, what this commitment to dialogue does mean is that students recognize and accept their responsibility as members of the community of learners gathered for the class, and appreciate their own authority. Active participation in dialogue assists students in seeing themselves as active meaning-makers and active agents in their own present and future contexts.

Dialogue facilitates learning as well as my understanding of how students are making sense of the material. This expectation of active participation through dialogue can be a dramatic shift for students. Often students are used to schooling experiences where teacher-talk predominates, is the sole voice of "authority," and always has the "correct" answer in mind.[4] Sometimes students struggle to present their ideas; I try to make it clear to students that although they need to be able to articulate their rationale for what they say, their ideas do not need to be "cleaned and pressed" before they are presented to the class. Learning takes place as we struggle together over ideas. The conversation is moved forward as students (and teacher) respond to questions and comments from the other members of the class.

Epilogue

> *It seems to me . . . that the real political task in a society such as ours*
> *is to criticize the working of institutions which appear to be both*
> *neutral and independent; to criticize them in such a manner that the*
> *political violence which has always exercised itself obscurely through*
> *them will be unmasked, so that one can fight them.*
> (Foucault, quoted in Rabinow, 1984, p. 6)

My project has been connected to the unmasking called for by Foucault. Unmasking is important as the dominant discourse of the discipline of educational psychology supports and advances social cognitions that make sense of many oppressive practices in such a way that they are frequently accepted as useful or at least tolerable. The discipline, embedded in its ideological inheritance, has not been able to address the ways its own knowledge claims and practices are caught in the web of meaning and power that mask oppression in education. Critical discourse analysis is a process of unmasking through an interrogation that disrupts this commonsense understanding and everyday practices of the discipline.

Critical discourse analysis as a research activity can be disorienting and disrupting. Yet, it is an important research enterprise because without this analysis social sciences may become part of a "social silence" (Fine, 1992) regarding society's "mechanisms of legitimization, marginalization, and punishment" (Brown, 1992, p. 223).

The present work is more about posing questions and critiques rather than offering solutions. This approach is not very satisfying to a modernist perspective. In fact, it may even be an irritant. However, questioning and critiquing as ways of looking at the discipline have had a profound influence on my own practice as a teacher-learner. There is so much that needs to be interrogated and contested, yet it is not for the sake of "science" or in the interest of advancing the discipline that I engage the discipline as I do. It is because the habits of thinking, the meaning-making system, and the practices of the discipline make a difference in the daily lives of children. It is a matter of compassion and social justice.

When teachers are simply trained to apply the mainstream tenents of the discipline to their practice, albeit with great expertise and sincerity, we assist students in fitting into the current system, not to question the system. Our students, our future teachers, may accept this system that fails so many children. Through a more critical examination of the discipline we question the way things are, we "make the familiar strange" and we accept the possibility that things can be different, that we can help to make things different.

Notes

Chapter 1. Multiple Readings of the Discipline of Educational Psychology

1. My use of quotation marks here, and frequently throughout this work, indicates irony. Quotation marks are also used to express a tension in using a word with shifting meaning.
2. Although I consider the mainstream, dominant discourse of the discipline of educational psychology to be oppressive and in need of critique, I am also aware that all discourse has the potential to be oppressive. Foucault has insisted that all discourses are potentially dangerous; he clarifies, "My point is not that everything is bad, but that everything is dangerous, which is not exactly the same as bad" (Foucault, quoted in Dreyfus & Rabinow, 1983, p. 231).
3. For a very helpful example of analyzing discourses as regimes of truth see Gore (1993).
4. Lenzo (1995) refers to someone who positions herself "within and against [her] field of study" (p. 21) as a "transgressive self." Issues of transgression are discussed in chapter 2.
5. The two texts are Gage and Berliner (1991) *Educational Psychology* and Woolfolk (1995) *Educational Psychology*.
6. By "classic" I mean those texts considered by members of the educational psychology community to contain the basic discourse of the field.
7. "Signification" is the process through which we make sense, how we come to make meaning or designate meaning. See Cherryholmes (1988) for a more complete analysis.
8. Foucault's understanding of "human sciences" includes what is usually considered the social sciences in this country as well as the humanities.

Chapter 2. Literature of Transgression

1. See Alison M. Jaggar's (1983) *Feminist Politics and Human Nature* for a discussion of what she sees as the four major contemporary feminisms (i.e., liberal, Marxist, radical, and socialist). Chris Weedon's (1987) *Feminist Practice and Poststructuralism* explains her thesis using explanations of liberal, radical, and socialist definitions of feminism.
2. I am referring here to a socialist perspective of feminism (Weedon, 1987) that views various oppressive structures (e.g., capitalism, patriarchy, racism) as interrelated.
3. This principle states that even the act of observation by a scientist will alter the results of an experiment.
4. I am grateful to Suzette Speight for pointing out that the connection of spirit with the mind and the masculine is not universally accepted. It exemplifies my own embeddedness in a Roman Catholic tradition.
5. The case of Rosalind Franklin's contribution to the model of DNA presented by James Watson is a perfect example. See A. Sayer (1975), *Rosalind Franklin & DNA* and J. D. Watson (1980), *The Double Helix: A Personal Account of the Discovery of the Structure of DNA.*

Chapter 3. Critical Educational Research

1. The term "modernity" does not allow a simple, uncontested definition. See Best and Kellner (1991); Giroux (1992); Sarup (1993); Usher and Edwards (1994) for helpful discussions. I appropriate Sarup's definition that modernity is used as "a summary term, referring to that cluster of social, economic and political systems brought into being in the West from somewhere around the eighteenth century onwards" (1993, p. 130).
2. The etymology of this word is very complex beginning with Comte's doctrine that only that which is accessible through the senses is positively knowable. Contemporary understanding of positivism links coming to know something objectively and truthfully through the utilization of the scientific method (Slife & Williams, 1997). See Giroux (1981) for a thorough critique.
3. "Postmodernism" as a term defies definition; thought to be at "once fashionable and elusive" (Sarup, 1993, p. 129), it is marked by a wide variety of interpretations. Usher and Edwards (1994) refer to postmodernism as a "loose umbrella term under whose broad cover can be encompassed at one and the same time, a condition, a set of practices, a cultural discourse, an attitude, a mode of analysis" (p. 7). See Best and Kellner (1991) for an explication of postmodern theory's historical development.
4. Foucault actually sees a postmodern critique as not contained in one epoch or another. Since power is "everywhere" so are disruptions to power-relationships. Discourse is always an incitement to discourse.
5. Gergen (1985) alerts readers to the interchangeable use of social "constructivism" and social "constructionism." He points out the Piagetian

origins of the former, as well as the former's use in reference to twentieth-century art. In order to avoid these confusions, I will use the latter form.

6. "Community" is an idea with a particular humanist value. While it is attractive, the interests of "community" can be used to marginalize and exclude voices from the conversation that raise difficult questions or subaltern discourses.

7. What is actually taught or learned in introductory educational psychology courses is not the issue here. However, the potential of textbooks to define the field is the issue.

8. Again, the use of quotes indicates my understanding of irony. Clear definitions of "student" and "teacher" are often blurred.

Chapter 4. Toward a Poststructuralist Analysis

1. This term has a complex etymology. It is used here in the sense of Antonio Gramsci (1971) to explain the dynamic of how some groups come to rule over other groups. Static and passive subordination is not the form of domination implied by this term. Rather, it "presupposes an active and practical involvement of the hegemonized groups" (Forgacs, 1988, p. 424). In other words, an important aspect of dominant groups maintaining their control and privilege is through the consent and support of other members of the society (Leistyna et al., 1996). van Dijk (1993) defines the term thus: "If the minds of the dominated can be influenced in such a way that they accept dominance, and act in the interest of the powerful out of their own free will, we use the term *hegemony*" (emphasis in the original, p. 255).

2. Freire (1992) insists that education that is liberatory must also be dialogic, thus "dialogue becomes a continuing aspect of liberating acting" (p. 134). The dialogue he is referring to is very different from everyday talk or conversation; it is "a process of learning and knowing [that] must always involve a political project with the objective of dismantling oppressive structures and mechanisms prevalent both in education and society" (Freire & Macedo, 1996, p. 203). See also chapter 6.

3. This work (Oakes, 1985) is itself problematic in that it uncritically theorizes from within a social reproductionist framework (see the discussion in Giroux & McLaren, 1989); still, Oakes's work has the potential of opening the debate regarding tracking. The example is presented here to illustrate how research that voices objections to mainstream perspectives can be marginalized and/or used in unintended ways, yet at the same time included in the text.

4. Gage and Berliner (1991) provide research studies that they interpret as meaning: "for most people intelligence begins to be stable by age 7. By age 12, intelligence is very stable. The rank order of individuals in intelligence at age 12 is much the same as their rank order at any subsequent age" (p. 58).

5. See Sapon-Shevin (1993) for a critical analysis of the educational, political, and justice issues in which the category "gifted student" is embedded.

6. Deevers (1995) has made the point of the necessity of turning to an examination of the discourse in order to understand why tracking procedures persist despite their harmful effects on students.

7. See Haymes (1996) for a helpful discussion of how psychology and biology are conflated so that regressive social cognitions can be perpetuated.

8. See Gore (1993) for an explanation of the use of the dash rather than the oblique stroke between "power" and "knowledge." I appropriate her use of the dash, as she explains the dash "holds the words together *and* apart, showing both their presupposition of each other and their difference from each other" (emphasis in the original, p. 51).

9. See, for example, Gould (1981) and Mensh and Mensh (1991).

10. A complete critique of how the construct of "intelligence" is developed in the mainstream discourse is important beyond the scope of this book. Many of the arguments regarding intelligence (i.e., able to be expressed as a single trait or "g," highly heritable, fixed, individuals can be ranked numerically) support the material in *The Bell Curve* (Herrnstein & Murray, 1994), including a defense of the fraudulent research practices of Cyril Burt. For a critique applicable to both texts see Fraser (1995); Gould (1981); Kincheloe, Steinberg, and Gresson (1996); and Mensh and Mensh (1991).

11. For example, both texts present Gardner's (1983) "multiple intelligences" and Sternberg's (1990) "triarchic theory."

12. I do not want to give the impression that there is a lack of resistance to the dominance of mainstream ideology. There is great resistance. There are regular interrogations by critical educational theorists and local resistances as well. The mainstream discourse, however, is unyielding to change.

Chapter 5. Disciplining the Discipline

1. The sense of the word "disciplining" in the chapter title was inspired by the title of Jana Sawicki's (1991) book, *Disciplining Foucault*. It is used here to highlight a major focus of the chapter, i.e., to subject the discipline to scrutiny.

2. Whereas Freire (1992) refers to "objects," Foucault (1995) refers to "subjects" of a "particular kind," i.e., docile and useful. There is irony here in that both words can convey similar meaning.

3. Shumway (1989) notes that this double meaning of "discipline" is sometimes considered as nothing more than an elaborate pun. However, Dreyfus and Rabinow (1983) explain that it is far from a "rhetorical convergence" as Foucault asserts that "the very self definition of the human science as scholarly 'disciplines' . . . is closely linked to the spread of disciplinary technologies" (p. 160).

4. Gage and Berliner (1991) report that these terms are no longer adequate or acceptable. However three categories are still used: "Although definitions vary by state, many federally funded programs are designed with three levels of mental retardation in mind. . . . Severely and profoundly mentally retarded . . . trainable mentally retarded . . . educable mentally retarded" (pp. 209–210).

5. Michelle Fine (1991) presents a helpful example in her work *Framing Dropouts*. In this work Fine allows the voices of "dropouts" to speak for themselves about their educational experiences. Their critical voices are juxtaposed against the voice of bureaucratic discourse that both silences them and excludes them from the educational system.

6. This is a reference to Carolus Linnaeus (1707–1778), the Swedish botanist, who originated binomial taxonomic classification.

7. See Hanson (1993) for a comprehensive discussion of the number and variety of tests available and used in the United States, in school settings and beyond.

8. Emotional and social development, as well as personality theory are offered as examples of "softer" areas (Ash & Love-Clark, 1985).

9. Emmer (1987) explains that *classroom management* and *discipline* are related because "management is chiefly directed at establishing conditions for good discipline" (p. 233). The terms are often used interchangeably.

10. See Sleeter and Grant (1994) for a comprehensive examination and analysis of various models of multicultural education. The "mosaic" metaphor, as well as "melting pot" is problematic.

11. Everhart's (1983) article is most helpful in showing the active construction of a subculture of student opposition to practices of classroom management. One of my students of educational psychology said in response to reading the article, "I never saw myself in print before."

12. All of students' behaviors may not appear disruptive (e.g., use of humor, avoidance, and various communication practices). Students learn both how to work the system and how to beat the system (Everhart, 1983).

13. Lewontin (1976) quotes Thorndike as saying that "the actual race of life . . . is not to get ahead, but to get ahead of somebody" (p. 107).

14. See, for example, Layzer (1975); Lewontin et al. (1996); Mensh and Mensh (1991).

15. It is added that the normal distribution "has been thoroughly analyzed by statisticians" (Woolfolk, 1995, p. 519). In light of the history of the development of this "normal" distribution it seems more correct to say that it has been thoroughly *constructed* by statisticians.

16. See Lewontin et al. (1996).

17. Even biology's conforming to normal distribution has been disputed. See Layzer (1976); Lewontin et al. (1996).

Chapter 6. Praxis

1. Again the reference to Freire's "object" and Foucault's "subject," see note 2 in chapter 5.
2. Silenced and marginalized voices are not to be romantized, however. They, too, are subject to critique.
3. The Sprinthall and Sprinthall (1990) textbook is a notable exception. This textbook is sprinkled with biographical profiles of many of the discipline's major developers.
4. Too much teacher-talk can have a silencing effect on students, yet this may not always be possible to avoid or even desirable to avoid at times. See Ira Shor (1992) for helpful insights on the effect of teacher-talk on critical dialogue in classrooms.

References

Anderson, L. M., Blumenfeld, P., Pintrich, P. R., Clark, C., M., Marx, R. W., & Peterson, P. (1995). Educational psychology for teachers: Reforming our courses, rethinking our roles. *Educational Psychology, 30*(3), 143–157.

Anyon, J. (1983). Workers, labor and and economic history, and textbook content. In M. W. Apple, & L. Weiss (Eds.), *Ideology and practice in schooling.* Philadelphia: Temple University Press.

Anzaldúa, G. (1987). *Borderlands/la frontera: The new mestiza.* San Francisco: Spinsters/The Aunt Lute Company.

Apple, M. W. (1988). *Teachers and texts.* New York: Routledge.

Apple, M. W. (1990). *Ideology and curriculum.* New York: Routledge.

Apple, M. W. (1993). *Official knowledge: Democratic education in a conservative age.* New York: Routledge.

Apple, M. W. (1994). Series editor's introduction. In A. Gitlin (Ed.), *Power and method: Political activism and educational research* (pp. 1–12). New York: Routledge.

Apple, M. W. (1995). Introduction. In M. Apple (Ed.), *Review of Research in Education* (Vol. 21 pp. xi–xviii). Washington, DC: American Education Research Association.

Apple, M. W. (1996). *Cultural politics and education.* New York: Teachers College Press.

Apple, M. W., & Christian-Smith, L. K. (1991). *The politics of the textbook.* New York: Routledge.

Aronowitz, S. (1988). *Science as power: Discourse and ideology in modern society.* Minneapolis: University of Minnesota Press.

Aronowitz, S. (1993). Paulo Freire's radical democratic humanism. In P. McLaren & P. Leonard (Eds.), *Paulo Freire: A critical encounter* (pp. 8–24). New York: Routledge.

Aronowitz, S., & Giroux, H. A. (1991). *Postmodern education: Politics, culture, and social criticism.* Minneapolis: University of Minnesota Press.

Ash, M. J., & Love-Clark, P. (1985). An historical analysis of the content of educational psychology textbooks. *Educational Psychologist, 20*(1), 47–55.

Bakhtin, M. M. (1981). *The dialogic imagination.* Austin: University of Texas Press.

Ball, S. J. (1990). Introducing Monsieur Foucault. In S. J. Ball (Ed.), *Foucault and education: Disciplines and knowledge* (pp. 1–10). New York: Routledge.

Banks, J. A. (1993). The canon debate, knowledge construction, and multicultural education. *Educational Researcher, 22*(5), 4–14.

Bauman, Z. (1991). *Modernity and ambivalence.* Ithaca, NY: Cornell University Press.

Bell, D. (1997). Protecting diversity programs from political and judicial attack. *The Chronicle of Higher Education, 43*(30), B4–B5.

Bensimon, E. A. (1995). Total quality management in the academy: A rebellious reading. *Harvard Educational Review, 64*(4), 593–611.

Berliner, D. C., & Calfee, R. C. (Eds.). (1996). *Handbook of educational psychology.* New York: Macmillan Library Reference.

Berliner, D. C., & Rosenshine, B. V. (Eds.). (1987). *Talks to teachers.* New York: Random House.

Berry, K. (1995). Students under suspicion: Do students misbehave more than they used to? In J. L. Kincheloe & S. R. Steinberg (Eds.), *Thirteen questions: Reframing education's conversations* (2nd ed.) (pp. 89–96). New York: Peter Lang.

Best, S., & Kellner, D. (1991). *Postmodern theory: Critical interrogations.* New York: The Guilford Press.

Bleier, R. (1984). *Science and gender.* New York: Pergamon Press.

Bleier, R. (1986). Lab coat: Robe of innocence or klansman's sheet? In T. de Laurentis (Ed.), *Feminist studies critical studies* (pp. 55–66). Bloomington: Indiana University Press.

Bloland, H. G. (1995). Postmodernism and higher education. *Journal of Higher Education, 66*(5), 521–559.

Blumenfeld, P. C., & Anderson, L. (1996). Editors' comments. *Educational Psychologist, 32*(1), 1–4.

Bowles, S., & Gintis, H. (1976). *Schooling in capitalist America.* New York: Basic Books.

Briscoe, F. M. (1993). Knowledge/power and practice: A Foucauldian interpretation of nineteenth century classrooms. Unpublished doctoral dissertation, University of Cincinnati, Cincinnati, Ohio.

Brown, R. H. (1992). *Writing the social text: Poetics and politics in social science.* New York: Aldine De Gruyer.

Burbules, N. C. (1995). Forms of ideology-critique: A pedagogical perspective. In P. L. McLaren & J. M. Giarelli (Eds.), *Critical theory and educational research* (pp. 53–70). Albany: State University of New York Press.

Burman, E. A. (1994). *Deconstructing developmental psychology.* New York: Routledge.

Burman, E., & Parker, I. (Eds.). (1993). *Discourse analytic research: Repertoires and readings of texts in action.* New York: Routledge.

Caputo, J. D., & Yount, M. (1993). Introduction. In J. D. Caputo & M. Yount (Eds.), *Foucault and the critique of institutions* (pp. 3–23). University Park: The Pennsylvania State University Press.

Carr, W., & Kemmis, S. (1986). *Becoming critical.* Philadelphia: The Falmer Press, Taylor & Francis, Inc.

Chall, J. S., & Conard, S. S. (1990). Textbooks and challenge: The influence of educational research. In D. L. Elliott & A. Woodward (Eds.), *Textbooks and schooling in the United States* (pp. 56–70). Chicago: The University of Chicago Press.

Cherryholmes, C. H. (1988). *Power and criticism: Poststructural investigations in education.* New York: Teachers College Press.

Collins, P. H. (1990). *Black feminist thought: Knowledge, consciousness, and the politics of empowerment.* New York: Routledge.

Cuban, L. (1984). *How teachers taught: Constancy and change in American classrooms: 1890–1990.* White Plains, NY: Longman.

Dales, B. L. (1992). *Power relations surrounding access to sources of information in public schools.* Unpublished doctoral dissertation, Miami University, Oxford, Ohio.

de Castell, S., Luke, A., & Luke, C. (Eds.). (1989). *Language, authority and criticism: Readings on the school textbook.* Philadelphia: The Falmer Press.

Deevers, B. (1995). Beyond tracking, what? Discursive problems and possibilities. In H. Pool & J. A. Page (Eds.), *Beyond tracking: Finding success in inclusive schools.* Bloomington, IN: Phi Delta Kappa Education Foundation.

Derry, S. J. (1992). Beyond symbolic processing: Expanding horizons for educational psychology. *Journal of Educational Psychology, 84*(4), 413–418.

Dewey, J. (1938). *Experience and education.* New York: Collier Macmillan Publishers.

Doyle, W., & Carter, K. (1996). Educational psychology and the education of teachers: A reaction. *Educational Psychologist, 31*(1), 23–28.

Dreyfus, H. L., & Rabinow, P. (1983). *Michel Foucault, beyond structuralism and hermeneutics.* Chicago: The University of Chicago Press.

Eisner, E. W. (1992). Are all causal claims positivistic? A reply to Francis Schrag. *Educational Researcher, 21*(5), 8–9.

Elliott, D. L., & Woodward, A. (1990). *Textbooks and schooling in the United States.* Chicago: The University of Chicago Press.

Emmer, E. T. (1987). Classroom management and discipline. In V. Richardson-Koehler (Ed.), *Educators' handbook a research perspective* (pp. 233–258). White Plains, NY: Longman.

Eribon, D. (1991). *Michel Eribon*. Cambridge, MA: Harvard University Press.

Everhart, R. B. (1983). Classroom management, student opposition, and the labor process. In M. W. Apple & L. Weis (Eds.), *Ideology and practice in schooling* (pp. 114–142). Philadelphia: Temple University Press.

Fairclough, N. (1995). *Critical discourse analysis: The critical study of language*. White Plains, NY: Longman.

Fancher, R. E. (1979). *Pioneers of psychology*. New York: W. W. Norton & Company.

Fancher, R. E. (1985). *The intelligence men*. New York: W. W. Norton & Company.

Fenstermacher, G. C. (1994). The knower and the known: The nature of knowledge in research and teaching. In L. Darling-Hammond (Ed.), *Review of research in education* (Vol. 20, pp. 3–56). Washington, DC: American Educational Research Association.

Fine, M. (1991). *Framing dropouts: Notes on the politics of an urban public high school*. Albany: State University of New York Press.

Fine, M. (1992). *Disruptive voices: The possibilities of feminist research*. Ann Arbor: The University of Michigan Press.

Forgacs, D. (Ed.). (1988). *A Gramsci reader*. London: Lawrence and Wishart Limited.

Foster, M. (1994). The power to know one thing is never the power to know all things: Methodological notes on two studies of black American teachers. In A. Gitlin (Ed.), *Power and method: Political activism and educational research* (pp. 129–146). New York: Routledge.

Foucault, M. (1972). *The archeology of knowledge*. New York: Pantheon Books.

Foucault, M. (1980a). Truth and power. In C. Gordon (Ed.), *Power/knowledge: Selected interviews and other writings* (pp. 109–133). New York: Pantheon Books.

Foucault, M. (1980b). The will to truth. In A. Sheridan (Ed.), *Michel Foucault: The will to truth* (pp. 113–134). New York: Tavistock Publications.

Foucault, M. (1980c). The eye of power. In C. Gordon (Ed.), *Power/knowledge: Selected interviews and other writings* (pp. 146–145). New York: Pantheon Books.

Foucault, M. (1981). The order of discourse. In R. Young (Ed.), *Untying the text* (pp. 48–79). Boston: Routledge & Kegan Paul.

Foucault, M. (1984). Politics and ethics: An interview. In P. Rabinow (Ed.), *The Foucault reader* (pp. 373–390). New York: Pantheon Books.

Foucault, M. (1988). Technologies of the self. In L. H. Martin, H. Gutman, & P. H. Hutton (Eds.), *Technologies of the self* (pp. 16–49). Amherst: The University of Massachusetts Press.

Foucault, M. (1990). *The history of sexuality*. New York: Vintage Books. (Original work published 1978)

Foucault, M. (1995). *Discipline & punish: The birth of the prison* (2nd ed.) New York: Vintage Books. (Original work published 1977)

Frankensteine, M., & Powell, A. B. (1994). Toward liberatory mathematics: Paulo Freire's epistomology and ethnomatics. In P. L. McLaren, & C. Lankshear (Eds.), *Politics of liberation: Paths from Freire*. New York: Routledge.

Fraser, N. (1989). *Unruly practices: Power, gender, and discourse in contemporary social theory*. Minneapolis: University of Minnesota Press.

Fraser, S. (Ed.). (1995). *The bell curve wars: Race, intelligence and the future of America*. New York: Basic Books.

Freire, P. (1985). *The politics of education*. New York: Bergin & Garvey Publishers, Inc.

Freire, P. (1992). *Pedagogy of the oppressed*. New York: Seabury Press. (Original work published 1970)

Freire, P., & Faundez, A. (1992). *Learning to question: A pedagogy of liberation*. New York: The Continuum Publishing Company.

Freire, P., & Macedo, D. P. (1987). *Literacy: Reading the word and the world*. South Hadley, MA: Bergin & Garvey Publishers, Inc.

Freire, P., & Macedo, D. P. (1996). A dialogue: Culture, language, and race. In P. Leistyna, A. Woodrum, & S. A. Sherblom (Eds.), *Breaking free* (pp. 199–228). Cambridge, MA: Harvard Educational Review. (Original work published 1995)

Gadotti, M. (1994). *Reading Paulo Freire*. Albany: State University of New York Press.

Gage, N. L. (1985). *Hard gains in the social sciences, the case of pedagogy*. Bloomington, IN: Phi Delta Kappa.

Gage, N. L. (1996). Confronting counsels of despair for the behavioral sciences. *Educational Researcher, 25*(3), 5–15, 22.

Gage, N. L., & Berliner, D. C. (1991). *Educational psychology* (5th ed.). Boston: Houghton Mifflin Company.

Gallagher, S. (1999). An exchange of gazes. In J. L. Kincheloe, S. R. Steinberg, & L. E. Villaverde (Eds.), *Rethinking intelligence: Confronting psychological assumptions about teaching and learning* (pp. 69–83). New York: Routledge.

Gardner, H. (1983). *Frames of mind: The theory of multiple intelligences*. New York: Basic Books.

Gergen, K. J. (1985). The social constructionist movement in modern psychology. *American Psychologist, 40*(3), 266–275.

Gergen, K. J. (1994). Exploring the postmodern: Perils or potentials? *American Psychologist, 49*(5), 412–416.

Giroux, H. A. (1981). *Ideology, culture, and the process of schooling*. Philadelphia: Temple University Press.

Giroux, H. A. (1983a). *Theory and resistance in education: A pedagogy for the opposition*. South Hadley, MA: Bergin & Garvey Publishers, Inc.

Giroux, H. A. (1983b, Winter). Ideology and agency in the process of schooling. *Journal of Education, 165*, 12–34.

Giroux, H. A. (1987). Introduction literacy and the pedagogy of political empowerment. In P. Freire & D. P. Macedo, *Literacy: Reading the word and the world* (pp. 1–27). South Hadley, MA: Bergin & Garvey Publishers, Inc.

Giroux, H. A. (1988). *Teachers as intellectuals.* New York: Bergin & Garvey.

Giroux, H. A. (1992). The hope of radical education. In K. Weiler & C. Mitchell (Eds.), *What schools can do: Critical pedagogy and practice* (pp. 13–26). Albany: State University of New York Press.

Giroux, H. A. (1995). Language, difference, and curriculum theory: Beyond the politics of clarity. In P. L. McLaren & J. M. Giarelli (Eds.), *Critical theory and educational research* (pp. 23–38). Albany: State University of New York Press.

Giroux, H. A., & McLaren, P. (1989). *Critical pedagogy, the state, and cultural struggle.* Albany: State University of New York Press.

Giroux, H. A., & McLaren, P. (1996). Teacher education and the politics of engagement: The case for democratic schooling. In P. Leistyna, A. Woodrum, & S. A. Sherblom (Eds.), *Breaking free: The transformative power of critical pedagogy.* Cambridge, MA: Harvard Education Review (Reprint Series No. 27). (Original work published 1986)

Giroux, H. A., & Purpel, D. (1983). *The hidden curriculum and moral education.* Berkeley: McCutchan Publishing Corporation.

Gitlin, A. D. (1990). Educational research, voice, and school change. *Harvard Educational Review 60*(4), 443–466.

Glover, J. S., & Ronning, R. R. (Eds.). (1987). *Historical foundations of educational psychology.* New York: Plenum Press.

Goodenow, C. (1992). Strengthening the links between educational psychology and the study of social contexts. *Educational Psychologist, 27*(2), 177–196.

Gordon, E. W., Miller, F., & Rollock, D. (1990). Coping with the communicentric bias in knowledge production in the social sciences. *Educational Researcher, 19*(3), 14–19.

Gore, J. M. (1993). *The struggle for pedagogies: Critical and feminist discourses as regimes of truth.* New York: Routledge.

Gottlieb, E. E. (1987). *Development education: Discourse in relation to paradigms and knowledge.* Unpublished doctoral dissertation, University of Pittsburgh.

Gould, S. J. (1981). *The mismeasure of man.* New York: W. W. Norton and Company.

Greene, M. (1994). Epistemology and educational research: The influence of recent approaches to knowledge. In L. Darling-Hammond, *Review of Research in Education* (Vol. 20, pp. 423–464). Washington, DC: American Educational Research Association.

Grinder, R. E. (1970). The crisis of content in educational psychology courses. *Educational Psychology, 8*(1), 4.

Grinder, R. E. (1989). Educational psychology: The master science. In M. C. Wittrock & F. Farley, *The future of educational psychology* (pp. 3–18). Hillsdale, NJ: Erlbaum.

Hanson, F. A. (1993). *Testing testing: Social consequences of the examined life*. Berkeley: University of California Press.

Haraway, D. (1988). Situated knowledges: The science question in feminism and the privilege of partial perspective. *Feminist Studies, 14*(3), 575–599.

Haraway, D. (1991). Situated knowledges: The science question in feminism and the privilege of partial perspective. In D. Haraway (Ed.), *Simians, cyborgs, and women: The reinvention of nature* (pp. 183–202). New York: Routledge. (Original work published 1988)

Haraway, D. (1991). *Simians, cyborgs, and women: The reinvention of nature*. New York: Routledge.

Haraway, D. (1996). Modest witness: Feminist diffractions in science studies. In P. Galison, & D. J. Stump (Eds.), *The disunity of science boundaries, contexts, and power* (pp. 428–441). Stanford: Stanford University Press.

Harding, C. G. (1985). Intention, contradiction, and the recognition of dilemmas. In C. G. Harding (Ed.), *Moral dilemmas philosophical and psychological issues in the development of moral reasoning* (pp. 43–55). Chicago: Precedent Publishing, Inc.

Harding, S. G. (1987). *Feminism and methodology: Social science issues*. Bloomington: University of Indiana Press.

Harding, S. G. (1991). *Whose science? Whose knowledge? Thinking from women's lives*. Ithaca, NY: Cornell University Press.

Harding, S. G. (Ed.). (1996). *The racial economy of science: Toward a democratic future*. Bloomington: Indiana University Press.

Harding, S. G., & O'Barr, J. F. (1987). *Sex and scientific inquiry*. Chicago: University of Chicago Press.

Haymes, S. N. (1996). Race, repression, and the politics of crime and punishment in the Bell Curve. In J. L. Kincheloe, S. R. Steinberg, & A. D. Gresson III (Eds.), *Measured lies* (pp. 237–251). New York: St. Martin's Press.

Herrnstein, R. J., & Murray, C. (1994). *The bell curve: Intelligence and class structure in American life*. New York: The Free Press.

Hilgard, E. R. (1996). History of educational psychology. In D. C. Berliner & R. C. Calfee (Eds.), *Handbook of educational psychology* (pp. 990–1004). New York: Macmillan Library Reference.

hooks, b. (1989). *Talking back*. Boston: South End Press.

hooks, b. (1990). *Yearning*. Boston: South End Press.

hooks, b. (1994). *Teaching to transgress: Education as the practice of freedom*. New York: Routledge.

Houtz, J. C., & Lewis, C. D. (1994). The professional practice of educational psychology. *Educational Psychology Review*, 6(1), 1–23.

Hubbard, R. (1989). Science, facts and feminism. In N. Tuana (Ed.), *Feminism and science*. Bloomington: Indiana University Press.

Hubbard, R., & Wald, E. (1993). *Exploding the gene myth: How genetic information is produced and manipulated by scientists, physicians, employers, insurance companies, educators, and law enforcers*. Boston: Beacon Press.

Jaggar, A. (1983). *Feminist politics and human nature*. Totowa, NJ: Rowman and Allanheld Publishers.

Jensen, A. R. (1987). Individual differences in mental ability. In J. S. Glover & R. R. Ronning (Eds.), *Historical foundations of educational psychology* (pp. 61–88). New York: Plenum Press.

Johnson, E. A. (1993). *Women, earth, and creator Spirit*. New York: Paulist Press.

Josselson, R., & Lieblich, A. (1996). Fettering the mind in the name of "science." *American Psychologist*, 51(6), 651–652.

Karier, C. J. (1972). Testing for order and control in the corporate liberal state. *Educational Theory*, 22(2), 154–180.

Keller, E. V. (1986). Making gender visible in the pursuit of nature's secrets. In T. de Lauretis (Ed.), *Feminist studies: Critical studies* (pp. 67–77). Bloomington: Indiana University Press.

Kessen, W. (1993). Rumble or revolution: A commentary. In R. H. Wozniak, & K. W. Fisher (Eds.), *Development in context: Acting and thinking in specific environments* (pp. 269–279). Hillsdale, NJ: Erlbaum.

Kincheloe, J. L. (1993). *Toward a critical politics of teacher thinking: Mapping the Postmodern*. Westport, CT: Bergin & Garvey.

Kincheloe, J. L. (1999). The foundationa of a democratic educational psychology. In J. L. Kincheloe, S. R. Steinberg, & L. E. Villaverde (Eds.), *Rethinking intelligence: Confronting psychological assumptions about teaching and learning*. New York: Routledge.

Kincheloe, J. L., & Steinberg, S. R. (1993). A tentative description of postformal thinking: The critical confrontation with cognitive theory. *Harvard Educational Review*, 63(3), 296–320.

Kincheloe, J. L., & Steinberg, S. R. (1999). Politics, intelligence, and the classroom: Postformal teaching. In J. L. Kincheloe, S. R. Steinberg, & L. E. Villaverde (Eds.), *Rethinking intelligence: Confronting psychological assumptions about teaching and learning* (pp. 337–345). New York: Routledge.

Kincheloe, J. L., Steinberg, S. R., & Gresson III, A. D. (Eds.). (1996). *Measured lies: The bell curve examined*. New York: St. Martin's Press.

Kincheloe, J. L., Steinberg, S. R., & Villaverde, L. E. (1999). *Rethinking intelligence: Confronting psychological assumptions about teaching and learning*. New York: Routledge.

Knorr-Centina, K., & Mulkay, M. (1983). *Science observed*. London: Sage.

Kohl, H. (1994). *I won't learn from you: And other thoughts on creative maladjustment*. New York: The New Press.

Kozol, J. (1991). *Savage inequalities: Children in America's schools*. New York: Harper Collins.

Kuhn, T. (1970). *The structure of scientific revolutions*. Chicago: The University of Chicago Press.

Lashgari, D. (1995). Introduction: To speak the unspeakable: Implications of gender, "race," class, and culture. In D. Lashgari (Ed.), *Violence, silence, and anger: Women's writing as transgression* (pp. 1–21). Charlottesville: University of Virginia Press.

Layzer, D. (1976). Science or superstition? A physical scientist looks at the IQ controversy. In N. J. Block & G. Dworkin (Eds.), *The IQ controversy* (pp. 194–241). New York: Pantheon Books.

Leistyna, P., Woodrum, A., & Sherblom, S. A. (Eds.) (1996). *Breaking free: The transformative power of critical pedagogy*. Cambridge, MA: Harvard Educational Review, Reprint Series No. 27.

Leitch, V. B. (1996). *Postmodernism—local effects, global flows*. Albany: State University of New York Press.

Lenzo, K. (1995). Validity and self-reflexivity meet poststructuralism: Science ethos and the transgressive self. *Education Researcher, 24*(4), 17–23.

Lewis, M. (1992). Power and education: Who decides the forms schools have taken, and who should decide? In J. L. Kincheloe & S. R. Steinberg (Eds.), *Thirteen questions: Reframing education's conversation* (pp. 39–64). New York: Peter Lang.

Lewontin, R. C. (1976). The analysis of variance and the analysis of causes. In N. J. Block & G. Dworkin (Eds.), *The IQ controversy* (pp. 179–193). New York: Pantheon Books.

Lewontin, R. C., Rose, S., & Kamin, L. J. (1996). IQ: The rank ordering of the world. In S. Harding (Ed.), *The racial economy of science*. Bloomington: Indiana University Press. (Original work published 1984)

Longino, H., & Doell, R. (1987). Body, bias, and behavior: A comparative analysis of reasoning in two areas of biological science. In S. Harding & J. F. O'Barr (Eds.), *Sex and scientific inquiry* (pp. 165–186). Chicago: University of Chicago Press.

Lorde, A. (1984). *Sister outsider*. Freedom, CA: The Crossing Press.

Luke, A. (1995). Text and discourse in education: An introduction to critical discourse analysis. In M. Apple (Ed.), *Review of Research in Education* (Vol. 21, pp. 3–48). Washington, DC: American Educational Research Association.

Luke, C., & Gore, J. (Eds.). (1992). *Feminisms and critical pedagogy*. New York: Routledge.

Lyotard, J. (1993). *The postmodern condition: A report on knowledge*. Minneapolis: University of Minnesota Press.

Macedo, D. (1994). *Literacies of power: What Americans are not allowed to know*. Boulder, CO: Westview Press, Inc.

Madigan, R., Johnson, S., & Linton P. (1995). The language of psychology: APA style as epistemology. *American Psychologist, 50*(6), 428–436.

Marshall, B. K. (1992). *Teaching the postmodern*. New York: Routledge.

Marshall, J. D. (1990). Foucault and educational research. In S. J. Ball (Ed.), *Foucault and education: Disciplines and knowledge* (pp. 11–28). New York: Routledge.

Mayer, R. E. (1992). Cognition and instruction: Their historic meeting within educational psychology. *Journal of Educational Psychology, 84*(4), 405–412.

Maxwell, J. A. (1992). Understanding and validity in qualitative research. *Harvard Educational Review, 62*(3), 279–300.

McLaren, P. (1989). *Life in schools*. White Plains, NY: Longman.

McNay, L. (1994). *Foucault: A critical introduction*. New York: The Continuum Publishing Company.

McNeil, L. (1983). Defensive teaching and classroom control. In M. W. Apple & L. Weis (Eds.), *Ideology and practice in schooling* (pp. 114–142). Philadelphia: Temple University Press.

Mead, G. H. (1934). *Mind, self, and society from the standpoint of a social behaviorist*. Chicago: The University of Chicago Press.

Mensh, E., Mensh, H. (1991). *The IQ mythology: Class, race, gender, and inequality*. Carbondale: Southern Illinois University Press.

Minh-ha, T. T. (1991). *When the moon waxes red: Representation, gender and cultural politics*. New York: Routledge.

Moke, P., & Bohan, J. S. (1992). Restructuring curriculum: Psychology's paradigm and the virtues of iconoclasm. *Women's Studies Quarterly 1&2*, 7–29.

Moraga, C., & Anzaldúa, G. (Eds.). (1983). *This bridge called my back: Writings by radical women of color*. New York: Kitchen Table; Women of Color Press.

Murphy, K. (1993). *Pedagogy for postmodernity: Travels in poststructuralism, feminism, and education*. Unpublished doctoral dissertation, University of Alberta, Edmonton, Alberta.

Namenwirth, M. (1986). Science seen through a feminist prism. In R. Bleier (Ed.), *Feminist approaches to science* (pp. 18–41). New York: Pergamon Press.

Neeley, S. (1996, November). It's the learning process, stupid! *Newsletter for Educational Psychologists, 20*(1), 1.

Oakes, J. (1985). *Keeping track: How schools structure inequality*. New Haven, NT: Yale University Press.

Olson, D. R. (1989). On the language and authority of textbooks. In S. de Castell, A. Luke, & C. Luke (Eds.), *Language, authority and criticism: Readings on the school textbook* (pp. 233–244). Philadelphia: The Falmer Press.

Peshkin, A. (1993). The goodness of qualitative research. *Educational Researcher, 2*(2), 24–30.

Peterson, B., & Tenroio, R. (1997). The Loss of Paulo Freire 1921–1997. *Rethinking Schools, 11*(4), 2.

Peterson, P. L., Clark, C. M., & Dickson, W. P. (1990). Educational psychology as a foundation in teacher education: Reforming an old notion. *Teachers College Record, 91*(3), 322–346.

Philp, M. (1985). Michel Foucault. In Q. Skinner (Ed.), *The return of grand theory in the human sciences* (pp. 65–82). New York: Cambridge University Press.

Popkewitz, T. S. (1992). Cartesian anxiety, linguistic communism, and reading texts. *Educational Researcher, 21*(5), 11–15.

Popkewitz, T. S. (1995). Foreword. In P. L. McLaren & J. M. Giarelli (Eds.), *Critical theory and educational research* (pp. xi–xxii). Albany: State University of New York Press.

Prado, C. G. (1995). *Starting with Foucault: An introduction to genealogy.* Boulder, CO: Westview Press.

Prawat, R. S., & Floden, R. E. (1994). Philosophical perspectives on constructivist views of learning. *Educational Psychology, 29*(1), 37–48.

Rabinow, P. (1984). (Ed.). *Foucault reader.* New York: Pantheon Books.

Randolph, C. H., & Evertson, C. M. (1994, Spring). Images of management for learner-centered classroom. *Action in Teacher Education,* 55–64.

Resnick, L. B., Levine, J. M., & Teasley, S. D. (Eds.) (1991). *Perspectives on socially shared cognition.* Washington, DC: American Psychological Association.

Restivo, S. (1988). Modern science as a social problem. *Social Problems, 35*(3), 206–225.

Rizvi, F. (1993). Children and the grammar of popular racism. In C. McCarthy & W. Crichlow (Eds.), *Race, identity, and representation in education.* New York: Routledge.

Rodriquez, R. (1983). *A hunger of memory: The education of Richard Rodriquez.* New York: Bantam Books.

Rosaldo, R. (1993). *Culture and truth: The remaking of social analysis.* Boston: Beacon Press. (Original work published 1989)

Rose, N. (1989). Individualizing psychology. In J. Shotter, & K. Gergen (Eds.), *Texts of identity* (pp. 119–132). London: Sage.

Rosenau, P. M. (1992). *Post-modernism and the social sciences.* Princeton, NJ: Princeton University Press.

Said, E. (1994). *Representations of the intellectual.* New York: Pantheon Books.

Salomon, G. (Ed.) (1995). Reflections on the field of educational psychology by the outgoing journal editor. *Educational Researcher, 30*(3), 105–108.

Sapon-Shevin, M. (1993). Gifted education and the protection of privilege: Breaking the silence, opening the discourse. In L. Weis & M. Fine (Eds.), *Class, race, and gender in United States schools* (pp. 25–44). Albany: State University of New York Press.

Sarup, M. (1993). *An introductory guide to post-structuralism and post-modernism* (2nd ed.). Athens: The University of Georgia Press.

Sarup, M. (1996). *Identity, culture, and the postmodern world.* Athens: The University of Georgia Press.

Sawicki, J. (1991). *Disciplining Foucault: Feminism, power, and the body.* New York: Routledge.

Sayer, A. (1975). *Rosalind Franklin and DNA.* New York: W. W. Norton & Company.

Scarr, S. (1985). Constructing psychology: Making facts and fables for our time. *American Psychologist, 40,* 499–512.

Scheurman, G., Heeringa, K., Rocklin, T., & Lohman, D. F. (1993). Educational psychology: A view from within the discipline. *Educational Psychologist, 28*(2), 97–115.

Scholes, R. (1985). *Textual power.* New Haven: Yale University Press.

Schon, D. A. (1983). *The reflective practitioner.* New York: Basic Books.

Schon, D. A. (1987). *Educating the reflective practitioner.* San Francisco: Jossey-Bass.

Schon, D. A. (1995, November–December). The new scholarship requires a new epistemology. *Change 27*(6), 12–25.

Schrag, F. (1992). In defense of positivist research paradigms. *Educational Researcher 21*(5), 5–15.

Sherif, C. W. (1987). Bias in psychology. In S. Harding (Ed.), *Feminism and methodology: Social science issues.* Bloomington: Indiana University Press.

Shor, I. (1992). *Empowering education: Critical teaching for social change.* Chicago: The University of Chicago Press.

Shuell, T. J. (1996). The role of educational psychology in the preparation of teachers. *Educational Psychologist, 31*(1), 5–14.

Shumway, D. R. (1989). *Michel Foucault.* Charlottesville: University Press of Virginia.

Silverman, N. (1991). From the ivory tower to the bottom line: An editor's perspective on college textbook publishing. In P. G. Altbach, G. P. Kelly, H. G. Petrie, & L. Weis (Eds.), *Textbooks in American society: Politics, policy, and pedagogy* (pp. 163–184). Albany: State University of New York Press.

Slavin, R. E. (1987). Ability grouping and student achievement in elementary schools: A best evidence synthesis. *Review of Educational Research, 57*(3), 293–336.

Sleeter, C. E., & Grant, C. E. (1994). *Making choices for multicultural education: Five approaches to race, class and gender* (2nd ed.). New York: Merrill.

Slife, B. D., & Williams, R. N. (1997). Toward a theoretical psychology. *American Psychologist, 52*(2), 117–129.

Smart, B. (1985). *Michel Foucault.* New York: Routledge.

Smith, D. (1987). Women's perspective as a radical critique of sociology. In S. Harding (Ed.), *Feminism and methodology: Social science issues.* Bloomington: Indiana University Press.

Smith, J. K. (1983). Quantitative versus qualitative research: An attempt to clarify the issue. *Educational Researcher, 12*(3), 6–13.

Soukhanov, A. H. (Ed.) (1984). *Webster's II new Riverside university dictionary.* Boston: Houghton Mifflin Company.

Soyland, A. J. (1994). *Psychology and metaphor.* London: Sage.

Speight, S., Myers, L. J., Cox, C. I., & Highlen, P. S. (1991). A redefinition of multicultural counseling. *Journal of Counseling and Development, 70*(1), 29–36.

Spring, J. (1991). Textbook writing and ideological management: A postmodern approach. In P. G. Altbach, G. P. Kelly, H. G. Petrie, & L. Weis (Eds.), *Textbooks in American society: Politics, policy, and pedagogy.* (pp. 185–198). Albany: State University of New York Press.

Sprinthall, N. A., & Sprinthall, R. C. (1990). *Educational psychology: A developmental approach* (5th ed.). New York: McGraw-Hill, Inc.

Squire, J. R., & Morgan, R. T. (1990). The elementary and high school textbook market today. In D. L. Elliott & A. Woodward (Eds.), *Textbooks and schooling in the United States* (pp. 107–126). Chicago: The University of Chicago Press.

Stanley, L., & Wise, S. (1993). *Breaking out again: Feminist ontology and epistemology.* New York: Routledge.

Star, S. L. (1991). Power, technology, and the phenomenology of conventions: On being allergic to onions. In J. Law (Ed.), *Power, technology and the modern world* (pp. 26–56). Oxford: Blackwell.

Sternberg, R. J. (1990). *Metaphors of mind: Conceptions of the nature of intelligence.* New York: Cambridge University Press.

Thomas, G. (1997). What's the use of theory? *Harvard Educational Review, 67*(1), 75–104.

Thomas, J. (1993). *Doing critical ethnography.* Newberry Park, CA: Sage.

Thorndike, E. L. (1910). *Education psychology.* New York: Teachers College Press, Columbia University.

Touraine, A. (1995). *Critique of modernity.* Cambridge, MA: Blackwell.

Usher, R. (1993). Re-examining the place of disciplines in adult education. *Studies in Continuing Education, 15*(1), 15–25.

Usher, R., & Edwards, R. (1994). *Postmodernism and education.* New York: Routledge.

van Dijk, T. A. (1993a). *Elite discourse and racism.* Newberry Park, CA: Sage.

van Dijk, T. A. (1993b). Principles of critical discourse analysis. *Discourse & Society, 4*(2), 249–283.

van Manen, M. (1990). *Researching lived experience: Human science for an action sensitive pedagogy.* Albany: State University of New York Press.

Walberg, H. J., & Haertel, G. D. (1992). Educational psychology's first century. *Journal of Educational Psychology, 84*(1), 6–19.

Watson, J. D. (1980). *The double helix: A personal account of the discovery of the structure of DNA.* (Ed. G. S. Stent). New York: W. W. Norton and Company.

Webb, N. (1995, July–August). The textbook business: Education's big dirty secret. *The Harvard Education Letter, XI*(4).

Webster's II new riverside university dictionary. (1984). Boston: Houghton Mifflin Company.

Weedon, C. (1987). *Feminist practice and poststructuralism.* New York: Basil Blackwell Inc.

Weiler, K. (1992). Introduction. In K. Weiler & C. Mitchell, *What schools can do: Critical pedagogy and practice* (pp. 1–10). Albany: State University of New York Press.

Weis, L., & Fine, M. (Eds.) (1993). *Beyond silences voices: Class, race, and gender in United States schools.* Albany: State University of New York Press.

Welch, S. D. (1990). *A feminist ethic of risk.* Minneapolis: Fortress Press.

Westbury, I. (1990). Textbooks, textbook publishers, and the quality of schooling. In D. L. Elliott & A. Woodward (Eds.), *Textbooks and schooling in the United States* (pp. 1–22). Chicago: The University of Chicago Press.

Wetherell, M., & Potter, J. (1992). *Mapping the language of racism: Discourse and the legitimation of exploitation.* New York: Columbia University Press.

Whatley, M. H. (1986). Taking feminist science to the classroom: Where do we go from here? In R. Bleier (Ed.), *Feminist approaches to science* (pp. 181–190). New York: Pergamon Press.

Willis, P. (1977). *Learning to labor.* Teakfield: Saxon House.

Wittrock, M. C. (1992). An empowering conception of educational psychology. *Educational psychologist, 27*(2), 129–141.

Woolfolk, A. (1995). *Educational psychology* (6th ed.). Boston: Allyn and Bacon.

Woolfolk Hoy, A. (1996). Teaching educational psychology: Texts in context. *Educational Psychologist, 31* (1), 41–50.

Woolgar, S. (1988). *Science: The very idea.* New York: Tavistock Publications Ltd.

Yee, A. H. (1970). Education psychology as seen through its textbooks. *Educational Psychology 8*(1), 4–6.

Young, M. J. (1990). Writing and editing textbooks. In D. L. Elliott & A. Woodward, *Textbooks and schooling in the United States* (pp. 71–86). Chicago: The University of Chicago Press.

Index

feminism, 27
  science and, 28, 32
feminist
  empiricism, 29
  scholarship, 21
  standpoint epistemology, 30, 66
Fenstermacher, G., 40, 43
Fine, M., 48, 115, 138, 144
Floden, R. E., 130
Foster, M., 60
Foucault, M., 2, 3, 4, 6, 8, 9, 10, 13,
    14, 46, 52, 53, 56, 61, 62, 82,
    83, 93, 94, 95, 96, 99, 100,
    101, 102, 104, 105, 106, 107,
    108, 109, 110, 124, 127, 129,
    137, 138, 141, 144
  genealogy and, 94, 99, 134
  methods of critique, 125
  normalization, 119, 120
  notion of archeology, 63
  power and, 18, 19, 93
  violence and, 22
Frankensteine, M., 126
Fraser, N., 18, 96
Freire, P., 8, 57, 58, 87, 93, 103, 126,
    127, 128, 129, 137, 142, 143

Gadotti, M., 127
Gage, N. L., 41, 43, 60, 61, 64, 68, 69,
    70, 71, 72, 73, 74, 76, 77, 78,
    79, 80, 84, 85, 86, 88, 89, 90,
    91, 103, 109, 111, 112, 114,
    115, 116, 117, 118, 119, 120,
    121, 122, 123, 124, 125, 140
Gallagher, S., 129, 133
Galton, F., 36, 139, 140, 141
geneology, 94, 99
Gergen, K. J., 8, 16, 40, 41, 43, 44,
    45, 47, 51, 63, 85, 86
gifted children, 80
Gintis, H., 117
Giroux, H., 8, 9, 10, 15, 39, 40, 44,
    45, 47, 51, 57, 60, 63, 66, 67,
    68, 69, 72, 73, 75, 77, 81, 87,
    88, 136, 142
Gitlin, A. D., 63
Glover, J. S., 53, 138, 139, 140
Goodenow, C., 130

Gordon, E. W., 43
Gore, J., 10, 65, 71, 87, 127
Gottlieb, E. E., 51
Grant, C. E., 88, 90
Greene, M., 37, 38
Grinder, R. E., 12, 68
Guthrie, R. V., 141

Haertel, G. D., 12
*Handbook of Educational Psychol-
    ogy* (Berliner and Calfee), 11
Hanson, F. A., 120
Haraway, D., 29, 31, 32, 48, 62, 95,
    107, 131
Harding, C. G., 22, 142
Harding, S. G., 22 26, 27, 28, 29, 30,
    31, 33, 58, 62, 87, 91, 131, 139
Harris, W. T., 97, 104
Hawthorne, N., 100
Haymes, S. N., 91
Heeringa, K., 53
Herrnstein, R. J., 41, 141
heteroglossia, 22, 23, 26, 33, 134
hierarchical observation, 94
Highlen, P. S., 35
Hilgard, E. R., 97
hooks, B., 2, 10, 22, 24, 25
Houtz, J. C., 54
Hubbard, R., 33, 34, 87
hypothetico-deductive scientific
    method, 40

ideology, 67
Immigration Act of 1924, 98
imperialism, 28
intelligence, 41, 81
intertextual reading, 57, 58, 134–36
intrinsic meaning structure, 44

Jensen, A. R., 98
Johnson, E. A., 35
Johnson, S., 16
Josselson, R., 48
juridico-political process, 98

Kamin, L. J., 97
*Keeping Track: How Schools Struc-
    ture Inequality* (Oakes), 79

Studies in the Postmodern Theory of Education

General Editors
Joe L. Kincheloe & Shirley R. Steinberg

Counterpoints publishes the most compelling and imaginative books being written in education today. Grounded on the theoretical advances in criticalism, feminism, and postmodernism in the last two decades of the twentieth century, Counterpoints engages the meaning of these innovations in various forms of educational expression. Committed to the proposition that theoretical literature should be accessible to a variety of audiences, the series insists that its authors avoid esoteric and jargonistic languages that transform educational scholarship into an elite discourse for the initiated. Scholarly work matters only to the degree it affects consciousness and practice at multiple sites. Counterpoints' editorial policy is based on these principles and the ability of scholars to break new ground, to open new conversations, to go where educators have never gone before.

For additional information about this series or for the submission of manuscripts, please contact:

> Joe L. Kincheloe & Shirley R. Steinberg
> c/o Peter Lang Publishing, Inc.
> 275 Seventh Avenue, 28th floor
> New York, New York 10001

To order other books in this series, please contact our Customer Service Department:

> (800) 770-LANG (within the U.S.)
> (212) 647-7706 (outside the U.S.)
> (212) 647-7707 FAX

Or browse online by series:

> www.peterlangusa.com